Saudi Arabia

The
Business Traveller's
Handbook

Andrew Mead

D1377804

The Grand Mosque in Makkah has been subject to wholesale renovation and extension since the 1990s. It is today larger than the entire city at the time of the Prophet. During the Hajj pilgrimage

The discovery of the reserves of 'black gold' came conveniently to Saudi Arabia at a time of need, but its impact has long surpassed anything the first prospectors imagined.

month alone, it commonly becomes the focus of over a million pilgrims from around the Islamic world.

King Saud University was opened in Riyadh in 1957 and has grown at a dramatic pace. The fountains of the atrium provide a breathtaking setting for the 24,000 students.

The Grand Mosque in Madinah is the second holiest mosque in Islam.

The road leaving Riyadh's King Khaled Airport is spanned by this magnificent arch.

The SABIC (Saudi Arabian Basic Industries Corp), based in Riyadh.

Riyadh's Kingdom Tower soars to 302 metres.

FOREWORD

Sir Andrew Green, KCMG
(Britain's Ambassador to Saudi Arabia 1996-2000)

Doing business in Saudi Arabia requires time, patience and a sound understanding of the market. Conditions are quite different from elsewhere in the Arab world, and different even from the Gulf countries. So this handbook is invaluable for the newcomer. Its author, Andrew Mead, has long experience of the country and his highly practical approach is exactly what is needed. He has, rightly, been careful to point to the important differences between the different regions of Saudi Arabia. Armed with his advice, most of the pitfalls should be avoidable, enabling the newcomer to join the ranks of the many businessmen who have conducted business successfully in the Kingdom.

The potential is considerable. Saudi Arabia is Britain's largest market in the Middle East. Exports in 1999 amounted to about £3 billion, split almost equally between goods and services. Britain is the third largest supplier to the Kingdom with just over 8 per cent of the market. The UK is also a major investor with over ninety joint ventures. New investment regulations in the Kingdom are designed to improve the investment climate and massive new foreign investment in the gas industry is expected over the next five to ten years. At the same time, the rapid growth in population can be expected to fuel the growth in the consumer market. British firms are present in every sector of the market.

Whatever your field, this Handbook will be a useful guide.

AG

CONTENTS

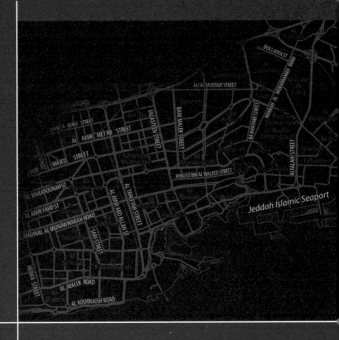

Saudi Arabia
yesterday and today

Saudi Arabia
yesterday and today

A bird's-eye view of the nation, its history and the special features that distinguish it internationally from other countries.

The modern country.

Overview

Geography

To many people in the western world, the Kingdom of Saudi Arabia is known only as an oil producing country located somewhere in the Middle East. Even the term 'Arabia' is sufficient in some quarters to conjure up romantic images of bearded strangers swathed in unfamiliar clothing riding camels through vast areas of barren sand. It is indeed true that Saudi Arabia possesses at least a quarter of the world's known oil reserves, and it does contain one of the world's largest deserts, but there is rather more to this remarkable kingdom than sand and oil.

The Kingdom occupies about 80 per cent of the Arabian Peninsula and has recently celebrated 100 years since its founding.

To the west, the Red Sea and the Gulf of Aqaba form a coastal border of almost 180 km stretching from Jordan in the north to the Yemen in the south. The northern border extends for about 1,400 kms from the Gulf of Aqaba in the west passing alongside Jordan, Iraq and Kuwait to Ras Al Khafji on the Arabian Gulf. In addition to the 300 kms or so of the eastern seaboard, Bahrain, Qatar and the United Arab Emirates abut the Kingdom and in the South the Sultanate of Oman and the Yemen occupy the southern areas of the peninsula. In addition to the principle land mass, Saudi Arabia also lays claim to many islands as well as some seabed areas beyond the 19 km limit.

Occupying approximately 2.3 million square kilometres (900,000 square miles) the Kingdom consists of several distinctive geographical areas. The western coastal plain, the Tihamah, whose width averages only 65 kms, extends along the Red Sea coastline and is bordered to its east by two mountain ranges. The northern half of the Red Sea escarpment is known as the Hijaz and seldom rises above 2,000 metres, but in the south the mountains of the Asir rise in places to over 3,000 metres. Both ranges drop steadily to around 600 metres in the Makkah region. The eastern side of the Asir slopes gently to a plateau which melds into the Rub al-Khali (or Empty Quarter), one of the largest sand deserts in the world, north of which lies the Najd.

The Najd region is mainly rocky plateau interspersed by small, sandy deserts and isolated mountain clumps.

Across the peninsula as a whole, the plateau slopes toward the east from an elevation of 1,360 metres in the west to 750 metres at its easternmost limit, marked by a ragged escarpment. A number of wadis cross the region in an eastward direction from the Red Sea escarpment toward the Arabian Gulf. There is little pattern to these remains of ancient riverbeds but the most important of them are Wadi ar-Rummah, Wadi as Surr, and Wadi ad-Dawasir. The heart of Najd is the area of the Jabal Tuwayq, an arc-shaped limestone ridge with a steep west face that rises between 100 and 250 metres above the plateau. A long, narrow strip of red desert sand known as the ad-Dahna separates Najd from eastern Arabia, which itself slopes eastward to the sandy coast along the Arabian Gulf.

Fault lines

Scientists analysing photographs taken by astronauts on the joint United States-Soviet space mission in July 1975 detected a vast fan-shaped complex of cracks and fault lines extending north and east from the Golan Heights. These fault lines are believed to be the northern and final portion of the Great Rift, which runs from the Mediterranean south through the Red Sea and Africa. They are presumed to be the result of the slow rotation of the Arabian Peninsula counter-clockwise in a way that will, in approximately 10 million years, close off the Arabian Gulf and make it a lake.

North of Najd a larger desert, the Great Nafud, isolates the heart of the peninsula from the steppes of northern Arabia. In the Nafud, a depression of immense dunes several kilometres in length and often 90 metres high, the Wadi as-Sirhan is an area almost 300 metres below the surrounding plateau and is believed to be the site of an ancient inland sea.

South of Najd lies the waterless Rub al-Khali and deep in the Rub al-Khali lies ad-Dahna an area, over 100 acres in size, covered with black glass, white rock and iron shards now recognised as perhaps the best-preserved and geologically simplest meteorite site in the world. East of the ad-Dahna lies the rocky Summan Plateau, a generally barren area dropping in elevation steadily until it abruptly changes to the flat lowland coastal plain. This area, about 60 kms wide, is generally featureless and covered with gravel or sand. In the north is the ad-Dibdibah gravelled plain and in the south the al-Jafurah sand desert, which reaches the gulf near Dhahran and merges with the Rub al Khali at its southern end. The coast itself is extremely irregular, merging sandy plains, marshes and salt flats with the sea. As a result, the land surface is unstable; in places water rises almost to the surface, and the sea is shallow, with shoals and reefs extending far offshore.

Rainfall

Saudi Arabia is one of the driest countries in the world, with no permanent rivers or lakes and rainfall averaging less than 13 cm per year. Marked seasons, in the western sense, do not exist. The climate is principally determined by the southerly shift in wind patterns during the winter months, which brings occasional rain and cool weather. Other factors such as latitude, proximity to the sea and altitude, also affect the climate. In the Empty Quarter, ten years may pass with no rain, yet in the southern Asir highland rainfall may exceed 255 mm per year and is generally dependable. Jeddah, on the shores of the Red Sea, has a hot and humid climate all the year round. Taif, on the other hand, and Abha, enjoy much more temperate weather.

Temperature

Summer is hot with temperatures in some areas reaching over 50°C. The proximity of the sea keeps temperatures in coastal areas more constant than in the interior where variations between day and night can be extreme. Sea breezes also bring moisture and the high humidity in coastal areas is in marked contrast to the arid interior. Winter months are cooler with an average temperature of 23°C in Jeddah and an average of 14°C in Riyadh. Temperatures can drop below freezing in the central and northern parts of the country and snow and ice sometimes occur in the higher elevations in the southwest. In areas where there is little ground cover, a northwesterly wind blows for most of the summer months and may, especially in the eastern part of the country, whip up violent sandstorms.

October to May is generally pleasant with cool nights and sunny days. From April to November, on the other hand, temperatures are considerably higher and life without air-conditioning would be unpleasant.

Ancient History

The Arabian Peninsula, including what we now recognise as the Kingdom of Saudi Arabia, has supported agricultural, herding and hunting cultures for thousands of years. Indeed to the south of the Kingdom, close to the Yemeni border, the town of Najran is thought to have been inhabited for about 4,000 years. Recent excavations of several archaeological sites in the Eastern Province have found evidence of earlier settlements, some of which may be over 7,000 years old.

Early civilisations

Surrounding cultures undoubtedly influenced the ancestors of today's Saudi Arabians. To the north the Sumerians created one of the earliest civilisations. There, the empires of Babylonia and Assyria rose and fell, as did that of Egypt to the west and northwest. The bodies of water on either side of the Arabian Peninsula provided relatively easy access to the neighbouring river-valley civilisations of the Nile and the Tigris-Euphrates and traders from China, India and East Africa left their mark in coastal areas. In the highland to the southwest the area was known to the Greeks and Romans as Arabia Felix (approximately 'Contented' or 'Blessed' Arabia), principally because of the legendary prosperity of the region as a source of incense and rosewater, and its dependable rains. It was also the legendary home of the Queen of Sheba. The climate and topography of this area permitted greater agricultural development than elsewhere in the country. Generous rainfall in Yemen enabled the people to feed themselves, while the exports of frankincense and myrrh brought riches to the area. As a result, civilisation developed to a relatively high level in southern Arabia by about 1000 BC.

Outside of the coastal areas, however, the harsh climate of the peninsula, combined with a desert and mountain terrain, limited agriculture and rendered access to the interior difficult. The population most likely subsisted on a combination of oasis farming and goat herding, with some portion of the society being partly nomadic. With the increasing domestication and exploitation of the camel, the conditions under which these people lived began to improve around 1000 BC. The camel was the only animal that could travel long distances over such harsh terrain with any reliability and the Arabs steadily began to benefit from some of the trade that had previously circumvented Arabia.

By about 500 BC, less than a century after **Nebuchadnezzar** had built the hanging gardens of Babylon, the Nabateans were emerging to dominate a northern area with its centre at Petra (now in Jordan). By the second century BC the southernmost stronghold of this territory was at **Madain Saleh** which is now in northwestern Saudi Arabia (about a 160km south of Tabuk). Evidence of their remarkable abilities to carve classical architecture out of the live rock still exists at the site today. Madain Saleh is the best known and the most spectacular archaeological site in Saudi Arabia. During its prime, it was an important stop on the caravan routes from the incense-producing areas of southern Arabia to Syria, Rome, and also to Egypt, Byzantium and beyond. The immense stone tombs, which have made it famous, were carved between 100 BC and AD 100. Medain Saleh was the second city in the Nabataean Empire.

The increased trans-Arabian trade brought the formation of small towns and cities, which developed within the Peninsula to service the requirements of the camel caravans. The most important of these was **Makkah**, birthplace of the **Prophet Muhammad**.

The Saudis, and many other Arabs and Muslims as well, trace much of their heritage to the birth of the Prophet. Muhammad was born in Makkah at a time when the city was flourishing as a trading centre, and for the residents of Makkah, tribal connections were still the most important part of the social structure. Muhammad was born into the Quraysh, which had become one of the leading tribes.

Tribes consisted of clans that had various branches and families, and Muhammad came from a respectable clan, but from a weak family situation. Mohammed's father Abd Allah had died before his son was born, leaving him without a close protector. As a child, he was sent to the desert for five years to learn the Bedouin ways that were slowly being forgotten in Makkah. He was fortunate, however, that his uncle Abu Talib was one of the leaders of the Hashimite clan which gave Muhammad a certain amount of protection when he began to preach against the authorities in Makkah.

Muhammad worked for Abu Talib in the caravan business which allowed him opportunities to travel and allowed contact with some of the Christian and Jewish communities that existed in Arabia. From these experiences he became familiar with the notion of scripture and the belief in one God. Despite this contact, tradition has it that Muhammad never learned to read or write.

Muhammad married a well-to-do widow when he was twenty-five years old; although he managed her affairs, he would occasionally go off by himself into the mountains that surrounded Makkah. He reports how, on one of these occasions, Muslim belief holds that the angel Gabriel appeared to him and told him to recite aloud. When Muhammad asked what he should say, the angel recited for him verses that would later constitute part of the Koran, which means literally 'the recitation.' Muhammad continued to receive revelations from God throughout his life, sometimes through the angel Gabriel and at other times in dreams and visions directly from God.

By 618 Muhammad had gained enough followers to alarm the city's leaders. The Quraysh hesitated to harm him because his uncle protected him, but they attacked those of his followers who did not have powerful family connections. To protect these supporters, Muhammad sent them to Ethiopia, where they were taken in by the Christian king who saw a connection between the Prophet's ideas and those of his own religion. Following his uncle's death in 619, however, Muhammad felt obliged to leave Makkah and in 622 he secretly left the city and travelled about 320km north to the town of Yathrib (Madinah). In leaving Makkah, Muhammad chose to quit the city where he had grown up to pursue his mission in another place. This emigration or *hijra* marks the beginning of the Islamic calendar, and consequently the foundation of Islam as a faith. The epoch prior to Islam is generally referred to as 'the time of ignorance' (*al-jahiliyyah*).

The Quraysh were unwilling to leave Muhammad in Yathrib, and various skirmishes and battles occurred, with each side trying to enlist the tribes of the peninsula in its campaigns. Muhammad eventually prevailed and in 630 he returned in triumph to Makkah, where he was accepted without resistance. The Prophet Muhammad's triumphal return to Makkah is emulated to this day by pilgrims celebrating the annual Hajj (or Pilgrimage).

By the time of his death in 632, Muhammad enjoyed the loyalty of all of Arabia.

The Holy Quran is believed by Muslims to contain the word of God revealed to the Prophet Muhammad over 20 years or more. Tradition has it that Muhammad caused some of these revelations to be written down on pieces of paper, stones, palm leaves, leather or whatever material was to hand. The revelations were also learned by heart by some of the companions and followers of Muhammad. Following the death of Muhammad in Madinah in 632 and after **the battle of Yamamah** in 633 in which large numbers of those who knew the revelations by heart were killed, it was feared that this knowlede would become lost. Accordingly it was decided to collate the revelations from all available written sources and 'from the hearts of the people'. A number of differing versions came into use and so it was that the Caliph Uthman (644-656) deputed a companion of the Prophet, Zayd bin Thabit, and other learned men to produce a revised version in consultation with those who could recite by heart the revelations. Thus came into being the definitive version of the Holy Quran.

After Mohammed's death, most Muslims acknowledged the authority of **Abu Bakr,** an early convert and respected elder in the community. Abu Bakr maintained the loyalty of the Arab tribes by force, and in the battles that followed the Prophet's death, which came to be known as the Apostasy wars, it became essentially impossible for an Arab tribesman to retain previous pagan beliefs.

Muhammad had no spiritual successor. There were, however, successors to his short-lived authority, and these were called Caliphs. For the first thirty years, caliphs managed the growing Islamic empire from Yathrib, which had been renamed Madinat an Nabi (the city of the Prophet) or al-Madinah al Munawwarah (the illuminated city). This is usually shortened simply to Madinah (the city).

Within a short time, the caliphs had established by conquest a large empire. With the conclusion of the

1

Apostasy wars, the Arab tribes united behind Islam and channelled their energies against the Roman and Persian empires. Arab-led armies pushed quickly through both of these empires and established Muslim control over an area extending from what is now Spain and Morocco to the Oxus and Indus of Pakistan.

The achievements of Islam were great and glorious, but from 656 onwards the growing empire was no longer controlled from Arabia. By the latter part of the seventh century the political importance of Arabia in the Islamic world had declined. Caliphs continued to rule the Islamic world from Damascus and then Baghdad until 1258 when the Mongols killed the last Caliph and all his heirs.

The Arabs

It is probably the nomadic people of the southern peninsula who were originally referred to as 'the Arabs', however many of these nomads migrated north over the centuries to the region known as the Fertile Crescent where they assimilated with both other travellers and the indigenous population. An 'Arab' today may be black or white, short or tall, blue eyed or brown and blond or dark haired; his ancestry obvious only in an analysis of his genes. Arabs today are probably best defined as those whose native tongue is Arabic.

Muslim civilisation remained vigorous for centuries, providing stability and advancing human knowledge when most of Western Europe was in a state of ferment and superstition known to historians as the Dark Ages. In the 13th century, the Mongol invasions dealt a devastating blow to the Arabs' eastern lands and their empire began to decline.

More Recent History

Historians generally agree to divide the more recent history of Saudi Arabia into three eras: The first period was from 1744 when **Sheikh Muhammad bin Abd al-Wahhab**, the founder of the 'back to basics' Islamic reform movement, came to Dir'iyyah in the lower Najd and joined with Muhammad Ibn Saud, Imam of the

House of Saud, in forming the First Saudi State. The followers of the reform movement and the House of Saud set out from their capital at Dir'iyyah to purify what they perceived to be the decadent Islam of the day and to embody God's law (the *Shari'a*) on earth. They created a central authority which over-rode previous tribal divisions and feuds in the name of a higher ideal. This First Saudi State was very successful and, in propagating its message, extended its influence over most of Arabia including the Holy Cities of Makkah and Madinah in the Hijaz.

By the time of Imam Saud's reign (1803-1814), the control that the religious reformers under the Saud family exercised in the Hijaz had dismayed the Ottoman Sultan who regarded himself as guardian of the Holy places. He urged his Viceroy in Egypt, Mohammed Ali Pasha, to see to the recapture of the Hijaz by Ottoman forces. After a series of inconclusive battles Makkah and Madinah were recaptured and, after a bloody campaign, during which Imam Saud, who died of a fever, and was succeeded by his son Abdullah, the Ottoman army conducted a savage invasion of the al-Saud homeland in Najd. This first period ended when the Turks took and destroyed Dir'iyyah in 1818 and Abdullah was sent in captivity to Istanbul where he was executed.

An Arab's property

John Lewis Burckhardt was a nineteenth century author of various books concerning his travels in Arabia. In one volume written early in the nineteenth century he wrote

'An Arab's property consists almost wholly in his horses and camels. The profits arising from his butter enable him to procure the necessary provisions of wheat and barley, and occasionally a new suit of clothes for his wife and daughters. His mare every spring produces a valuable colt, and by her means he may expect to enrich himself with booty. No Arab family can exist without one camel at least; a man who has but ten, is reckoned poor; thirty or forty, place a man in easy circumstances; and he who possesses sixty, is rich.'

The second era began in 1824, the year in which **Imam bin Turki bin Abdullah** liberated the Najd region from Muhammad Ali Pasha. The al-Saud gradually resumed their dominance of the central Najd region with Riyadh now the capital only to be superseded in the 1890s by the al-Rashid, who originated in Hail, northwest of Riyadh. The period ended when Imam Abdul Rahman, the head of the Al-Saud, was forced to abandon Riyadh and seek refuge in Kuwait in 1891. It was in Kuwait that the young **Abdul Aziz**, the 12-year-old son of Abdul Rahman grew up and gained the experience and knowledge which enabled him to embark on the third era; the return of the al-Saud to the Najd at the beginning of the twentieth century.

The followers of Abd al-Wahhab

In his *Notes on the Bedouins and Wahabys* published early in the 19th century, John Lewis Burckhardt wrote 'respecting the Wahabys, various contradictory and erroneous statements have been given in the few accounts hitherto published.' He went on to record, 'By unwearied exertions and efforts, Abd el Azyz and Ibn Saoud, the son and grandson of the first leader Mohammed, succeeded in carrying their arms to the remotest corners of Arabia: and while they propagated their religious tenets, they established a supremacy of power comfortably with these tenets, which taught the Arabs to acknowledge a spiritual and temporal leader in the same person, as they had done on the first promulgation of Islam.'

After a daring and dramatic capture of Riyadh's fortress in a dawn raid in January 1902, Abdul Aziz 'Ibn Saud' and his allies defeated the Rashidi forces in a series of battles, gradually winning control of the remaining settled areas of Najd. Although Ottoman forces equipped with artillery combined with the Rashidi armies, they could not prevent Abdul Aziz from consolidating his mastery over all central Arabia by the middle of the first decade of the twentieth century. Taking advantage of the crumbling Ottoman Empire and the weakening of Turkish garrisons on the peninsula, Abdul Aziz invaded the Eastern Province in 1913 and then the entire gulf coast between Kuwait and Qatar after overcoming the Turkish garrison at Hofuf. Subsequent success included control over the region encompassing Qatif and Jubail and in 1915 relations with the British were established through their agent in Kuwait, Captain Shakespear. In 1921 the northern city of Hail was overcome, and in 1924 the Holy City of Makkah was relieved of its Hashemite rule and gathered into the Saudi fold. Madinah and Jeddah followed suit and in 1925 Abdul Aziz proclaimed himself King of Hijaz as well as Sultan of Najd. In 1927 the new name of the country became 'The Kingdom of Hijaz and Najd and their Dependencies' and in 1930 the Asir was added to this ever-expanding state. In 1932 the union of Najd, Hijaz, Asir and al-Hasa was officially renamed the Kingdom of Saudi Arabia.

Notwithstanding the role of the Ottoman Empire, most of the peninsula had been almost a world unto itself until the tribes were drawn into larger outside conflicts during the First World War. Relying on the Ottomans to maintain stability in the Middle East before the war, Britain had disdained a pact with Abdul Aziz, but on Turkey's adherence to the German cause followed by Britain's declaration of war against the Ottoman Empire in October 1914, the British sought an alliance with the House of Saud. By a treaty signed in December 1914, the British recognised Saudi independence and provided Abdul Aziz with financial subsidies and weapons in the form of small arms. As his part of the agreement, Abdul Aziz promised to keep 4,000 men in the field against the House of Rashid, which was aligned with the Ottomans. Following defeat in the First World War, the Ottoman Empire ceased to exist.

King Abdul Aziz died in November 1953. He was succeeded by **King Saud** who followed the course of action established by his father. In 1964, for reasons of health, he conceded power to his half-brother Faisal who achieved considerable economic and political stability in the Kingdom, and stable international relations. **King Faisal** was assassinated by a deranged relative in 1975, and was succeeded by his half-brother King Khalid who in turn entrusted many affairs of state to his brother, the then Crown Prince Fahd bin Abdul Aziz and next half-brother in line to the throne.

1

Fahd was born in Riyadh in 1921 and was appointed the first Saudi Arabian Minister of Education in 1953. He served at that Ministry for five years, laying the foundations for the Kingdom's ambitious educational programme. He became Minister of the Interior in 1962, holding this position for 13 years and, by 1975, when he became Crown Prince, he had undertaken the supervision of both the planning and the implementation of the Kingdom's second and subsequent Five-Year Plans.

On King Khalid's death in 1982 the crown passed to the Crown Prince. On **King Fahd**'s accession, a royal decree, appointed HRH Prince Abdullah bin Abdul Aziz to be Crown Prince in addition to his post as Commander of the National Guard. Prince Abdullah today carries the title Prince Regent. HRH Prince Sultan bin Abdul Aziz, the Minister of Defence and Aviation, was appointed Second Deputy Premier.

Styled 'the Custodian of the two Holy Mosques', King Fahd Abdul Aziz al-Saud was born in Riyadh in 1921. He was appointed the first Minister of Education in the Kingdom in 1953 and in 1962 became Minister of the Interior. Since attaining the throne, King Fahd has engaged in implementing the successive development plans that have enabled the Kingdom to establish the high levels of modernisation prevailing today.

The system of government is described as an Islamic monarchy where the King is the Prime Minister and leader of prayer and religious matters. The constitution is based on the Holy Quran and the traditional sayings of the Prophet Mohammed. The King is also Commander-in-Chief of the Armed Forces and in the final analysis all ministries and government agencies are responsible to his authority. Successive Saudi kings have developed a centralized system of government. The King is guided by a Council of Ministers. Access to the King and other highly-placed individuals is through the well-established *majlis* or public audience. The Majlis Al Shura, or Shura Council, was expanded to 90 members in 1997, 120 members in 2001 and to 150 members in 2005 and advises the Council of Ministers on matters pertaining to government programmes and policies.

The Kingdom is divided into 13 provinces, through which local affairs are administered. Each province is headed by a Governor, appointed by the King. In 2005, limited local elections were held for half the members of the 178 municipal councils.

Modern Times

With the discovery of oil in March 1938, the fortunes and lifestyle of the people of Arabia changed dramatically. From almost inconsequential beginnings at the turn of the twentieth century, the House of Saud has grown to become one of the most influential ruling families in the world.

The discovery of oil

With the economy financed by oil, the pace of growth and change has been phenomenal. With the wholesale revision of relations with the commerical oil giants in October 1979, and with the massive hike in the price of oil, Saudi Arabia opened its wallet to the world over the course of the 1970s and set in train three decades of gigantic infrastructure projects. Since 1990 oil prices have fluctuated considerably and measures have been taken to decrease the Kingdom's reliance on oil revenues. The Saudi Government has stated its recognition that the private sector needs to become the engine of economic growth but even though oil still accounted for about 36 per cent of GDP in 1999 it had grown to about 40 per cent by 2005. Saudi net export oil revenues for 2006 are forecast to be in the region of $154 billion. The Government sector has accounted for approximately 26 per cent of GDP but it is worth bearing in mind that the giant petrochemical company SABIC (Saudi Arabian Basic Industries Corporation) is counted as part of the private sector, although 70 per cent state owned.

Population

Critical to the economic fortunes of the Kingdom is the rate of change in population growth. Estimates vary, but the Saudi population is numbered at about 24 million in 2006 including as many as 7 million expatriates mostly from neighbouring Arab or Muslim countries. The growth rate was estimated in 2000 at about 3.34 per cent per annum but according to the CIA *World Factbook* had fallen to 2.31 per cent by 2005. With labour force estimates of about 2.8 million Saudis and 4.7 million non-Saudis it does not need a super-computer to see that unemployment amongst Saudi youth will be a major challenge to central government in the not too

1

distant future. Over half the Saudi population is currently under 18 years of age and hundreds of thousands of them will emerge onto the job market each year. The expansion of government related jobs has all but ceased and whilst the private sector is increasing in importance, much of the expansion is in highly capital-intensive areas where job creation is minimal. Official unemployment figures are not available but commentators on the economy suggest that estimated figures of 13 per cent unemployment amongst Saudis in 1997 may have increased to 30 per cent by 2003.

In dealing with this challenge, the Government has instituted a policy of substituting Saudis for foreigners. This 'Saudisation' of the labour force is propelled by regulations requiring companies to increase the percentage of Saudi employees each year. Other regulations have defined certain job categories that may only be occupied by Saudis. In 2003 for example a decision was taken banning all foreigners from working in Jewellery shops, which was supposed to create 20,000 job opportunities for Saudis. The success of this programme is limited however by the numbers of those suitably qualified and those who are willing to do the work offered.

Saudisation of the labour force

The Kingdom's strategic location and its oil reserves have made its friendship of prime importance to western countries. Military co-operation, for example, during the 1991 Gulf War was extensive. This has not always suited many sectors of the population who blame the West for many of Saudi Arabia's problems. According to the 9/11 Commission Report issued in 2004, 15 of the 19 hijackers deemed responsible for the deaths of over 3000 people on that fateful day were Saudis. In December 2004, a Saudi branch of Al-Qaeda posted a message on its website urging its members to 'strike all foreign targets and the hideouts of the tyrants to rid the peninsula of the infidels and their supporters.'

Military co-operation

Terrorist attacks on Westerners and Western interests in Saudi Arabia since 2000 have shaped the lifestyle of ex-patriots and that of business visitors whose regularity of visits has fallen significantly. Despite many of the sensationalist headlines, Saudi Arabia has made striking improvements with its internal security issues and the Kingdom is seen as relatively safe.

Saudi Arabia became the 149th member of the World Trade Organisation on 11 December 2005. As the world's 13th largest exporter and the 23rd largest importer it had taken 12 years for membership to be granted. The Saudis continue to revise their business laws in order achieve compliance with WTO rules.

In a speech to the Gulf Co-operation Council in December 1998 HRH The Prince Regent Abdullah is reported to have said 'the boom days are over'. In many business sectors however the boom appears to be continuing. In the mobile phone sector for example, growth in Saudi in 2005 was reported at 30 per cent compared to a worldwide average of 23 per cent.

Whilst there are undoubted and significant opportunities for foreign companies to do business in Saudi Arabia, there are constant changes in regulations which could effect the trading climate. Readers are recommended to seek professional advice before entering into any new business venture.

government could reduce its current level of debt by involving private finance in certain public areas.

In a speech to the Gulf Co-operation Council in December 1998 HRH The Prince Regent Abdullah is reported to have said 'the boom days are over'. Whilst there are undoubted and significant opportunities for foreign companies to do business in Saudi Arabia, there are constant changes in regulations which could effect the trading climate. Readers are recommended to seek professional advice before entering into any new business venture.

2

Investigating the potential market

investigating the potential market

An outline of some of the myriad organisations which exist to assist the businessman or woman, along with an assessment of their focus and likely relevance.

Sources of Information

The business traveller should, of course, be as well informed as possible before entering a new market. This section acts as a guide to where to find this information. It includes government and private sources in electronic and hardcopy format. This section also discusses the availability of reliable market and economic information.

Whether you are visiting Saudi Arabia for the first time or making the latest in a series of regular visits, preparation is essential to get the most out of the trip and ensure that your project succeeds. Obtaining the latest information will allow you to plan effectively for your trip, get a clear picture of the market you are entering, identify any trends or opportunities that you can use to your advantage and spot any pitfalls. It is equally important to ensure that the information you use is accurate and that you are aware of any possible bias.

Saudi Arabia is not a country that is easy for businessmen to dip in and out of. To get best results from the market you will need to show a long-term commitment to business relationships in the Kingdom. Do not expect to gain an instant understanding of the market or instant results. The sources below can provide a starting point for research on the Saudi market and many of them are free or provide information at very little cost. The information thus gained will provide a good overview of the market.

Saudi Arabian Embassies

UK

Royal Embassy of Saudi Arabia
15 Curzon Street
London W1

❏ Tel: +44 20 7917 3000 (main switchboard); +44 20 7917 3089 (press office) Fax: +44 20 7917 3088

The Saudi Commercial Office, which is part of the Embassy, provides companies, organisations and individuals with trade, economic and statistical data, and advises on sources of detailed market information about the Kingdom.

❏ Tel: +44 20 7917 3441 Fax: +44 20 7917 3161

The Saudi Information Centre, which is separately located at 18 Cavendish Square, provides more general

2

information about Saudi Arabia for all interested parties. An assortment of newspapers, books, pamphlets and videos are available for reference and distribution.

❏ Tel: +44 20 7629 8803 Fax: +44 20 7629 0374

US

Royal Embassy of Saudi Arabia
601 New Hampshire Avenue, NW
Washington DC 20037

❏ Tel: +1 202 342-3800
+1 202 337-4088 (Commercial Office)
+1 202 337-4134 (Information Office)
+1 202 342-7393 (Medical Office)
+1 202 342-3800 (Visa Section)

Canada

Royal Embassy of Saudi Arabia
Suite 901
Ottawa
Ontario
Canada K1T 6B9

❏ Tel: +1 613 237 4100 Fax: +1 613 237 0567

The addresses of Saudi Arabian Embassies in other countries are contained in Appendix 1.

Ministries and other Government Agencies

UK

The primary British government source for information on overseas markets is UK Trade & Investment (UKTI). Unlike in the 1980s and 90s when country desks were staffed by a host of specialists, the Desk Officer may now have to deal with several countries in the region and most enquirers will be directed to the UKTI website at www.uktradeinvest.gov.uk where a range of reports concerning different market sectors can be downloaded.

The website also offers links to a range current business opportunities which are regularly updated by staff from the in-country British Embassy offices. In addition, a system of email alerts can be personalised for your own area of interest.

International Trade Teams are based throughout England. To locate your nearest team, you will need to visit the website and enter your postcode or call +44 20 7215 8000. If you are in Scotland, Wales or Northern Ireland, you will be given contact details for the appropriate national government agency. See below for regional details.

From the initial contact you will be directed to an International Trade Adviser (ITA) who can provide you with essential and impartial advice on all aspects of international trade including financial subsidies, export documentation, contacts in overseas markets, overseas visits, translating marketing material, e-commerce, subsidised export training and market research. Every UK region also has dedicated sector specialists who can provide advice tailored to your industry. With more than 40 offices in the UK, based in partner organisations such as Business Links, Chambers of Commerce and Regional Development Agencies the range of assistance offered is vast.

For new and inexperienced exporters, a programme called 'Passport to Export' will take you through the mechanics of exporting. An online checklist 'Are You Ready to Export?' will give you a better idea of your company's export capabilities and help to identify areas for improvement. On completing the checklist you will be provided with an export readiness report. This can also be sent to a Business Link, who will contact you if required to discuss how UKTI can help your business.

The contact details for UKTI, Saudi Arabia desk are:

Kingsgate House
66-74 Victoria Street
London, SW1E 6SW

❏ Tel: +44 207 215 4839 Fax: +44 207 215 4831;
Website: www.uktradeinvest.gov.uk/ukti/saudi_arabia

The DTI operates an excellent, free library for exporters. You can find an extensive range of publications on Saudi Arabia and most other countries including directories, the latest Economist Intelligence Unit reports and country guides.

2

Export Market Information Centre
Kingsgate House
66-74 Victoria Street
London SW1E 6SW

❑ Tel: +44 20 7215 5444 Fax: + 44 20 7215 4231
Email: EMIC@xpd3.dti.gov.uk

Website: www.brittrade.com/emic

Another source of assistance, which is totally free to the potential British exporter, is the **Export Promoter.** In 1995 the Secretary for State for Industry, Michael Heseltine and his Minister for Trade, Richard Needham, launched an initiative to promote British exports. They proposed to second up to 100 people from British industry who were specialists in either certain countries or certain disciplines. These Export Promoters (EPs) are seconded to the DTI from British Industry for a period of up to three years. The majority of these experts are businessmen with particular knowledge of particular countries. In a few cases the promoter is an industry specialist e.g. environment, power etc. Export Promoters (EPs) can be contacted by anyone. They are likely to be frequent visitors to their countries of responsibility and will have a lot of information relating to opportunities, agents, partners, exhibitions, trade missions etc. They can generally be found through the country desk officer at Trade Partners UK at Kingsgate House. They may not be at Kingsgate House since many either work from home or are attached to one of the regional DTI offices. These EPs are not only expected to be well informed but also to be 'honest' and able to give direct answers about their markets and whether an opportunity for a particular company might exist. Their time and assistance is free and they will usually be able to help a company with introductions and contacts at the highest level – they have a reporting line directly to the minister for trade in the UK. Overseas they work closely with the Commercial section of the Embassy.

Since Export Promoters are, through the nature of their secondment, likely to change regularly, so it is best to contact the office above for the current EP's contact details.

In the UK, support includes access to the TradeUK Export Sales Lead Service and National Exporters Database and Grant-Supported Trade Fairs and Exhibitions. Contacts for first-time exporters are:

England. One of the network of Business Links
❏ Tel: +44 345 567765 or visit the Business Link
Signpost website at www.businesslink.co.uk

Scotland. Scottish Trade International
❏ Tel: +44 9141-228 2812/2808 or www.sti.org.uk

Wales. Welsh Office Overseas Trade Services
❏ Tel: +44 1222 825 097 or www.wales.gov.uk

Northern Ireland. Industrial Development Board for
Northern Ireland
❏ Tel: +44 2890 233233 or www.idbni.co.uk

The Committee of Middle East Trade (COMET) is a
Trade Partners UK advisory group for the Middle East.
Its main purpose is to assist in the formulation of
Government trade policy and to seek out and promote
ways of improving UK performance in the region acting
as an interface between industry and government. Its
staff can provide briefing for UK firms on individual
Middle East markets and can advise on more specialised
information sources available to the exporter. Under a
restructuring exercise late in 2000, COMET's function
was largely absorbed by the Middle East Association
(*see p.44*).

COMET

The Committee of Middle East Trade (COMET)
Bury House
33 Bury Street, St James's
London SW1Y 6AX
❏ Tel: +44 20 7839 1170/1191 Fax: +44 20 7839 3717
Website: www.comet.org.uk
Email: enquiries@comet.org.uk

Credit Guarantees

ECGD or the **Export Credits Guarantee Department** is
also associated with the DTI, but is self supporting. The
services offered by this organisation are very specialised
and complex but, essentially, it operates a scheme to
insure overseas investments made by British business
organisations. It is an arguable point that if ECGD cover
is available then the risk involved is minimal and that it
might be better to save the premiums. ECGD can,
however, offer some methods for a prospective client to
defer payments to an exporter. The facility can have its
attractions.

2

One of the most common ways in which ECGD becomes involved with an export is through a line of credit. When a UK bank offers a facility to an overseas bank to enable goods or services to be purchased from the UK, ECGD can insure that risk. The loan facility is used to pay the exporter once the goods have been exported or the service performed. If the borrower fails to repay any part of the loan then the UK bank is covered by the ECGD guarantee. Overseas investment insurance is also available.

ECGD
PO Box 272, Aldermanbury House
Aldermanbury, London, EX2P 3EL

❑ Tel: +44 20 7512 7000 / +44 20 7382 7000
Email: help@ecgd.gov.uk

Website: www.open.gov.uk/ecgd

Military Sales

Advice on military sales and eguipment can be obtained from a specialist organisation in London, the **Defence Export Sales Organisation** (DESO), part of the Ministry of Defence. This is a very active export service manned by senior diplomats on temporary secondment to DESO. The business is, of course, highly specialised, and overseas is not handled by the embassy commercial offices but by the defence attachés. Defence sales include obvious military hardware and equipment but also includes the construction of airfields, supply of 4x4 vehicles and uniforms, etc. DESO will also advise on any relevant political sensitivities.

DESO
Ministry of Defence
Metropole Building
Northumberland Avenue
London WC2N 5BL
❑ Tel: +44 20 7218 9000 Fax: +44 20 7807 8307

Other Ministries

UK

The UK Ministry of Education does not take an active part in promoting the export capabilities of its associated industries; this task is undertaken by the **British Council.** The Council is responsible for promoting British Culture overseas and is very active in supporting UK educational and cultural enterprises. The Council, with offices across the UK, is financially self-supporting and has, therefore, perhaps reluctantly at first, entered into the world of commerce. It has officers responsible for exports and for liaison with other government bodies.

British Council: ❑ Tel: +44 20 7389 4141
Website: www.britcoun.org or newweb.britcoun.org

Two other ministries which promote British exports are the ministries of agriculture and health. The export departments in these have specialised sector information freely available to any business people. Overseas visits by ministers and officials accompanied by business people are frequently arranged.

Ministry of Health: www.gov.uk
Ministry of Agriculture: www.maff.gov.uk

In general, all UK government offices can be found at www.open.gov.uk

The European Union

The most relevant office of the European Union (EU) is **Directorate General 1** (DG1) which deals with trade and political matters; it is based in Brussels and has overseas representative offices. DG1 also controls the **European Community Investment Partners** scheme (ECIP), finance for the region and relations with the European Investment Bank (EIB). DG1 has country desks, much the same as Trade Partners UK and the Foreign and Commonwealth Office (FCO), with desk officers, who can offer information and assistance.

FCO

Funds are available from the Union for various development programmes apart from direct project finance, including money for companies to set up partnerships and/or joint ventures. The ECIP scheme can assist with finance to form such a joint venture and for training of personnel. ECIP can also finance feasibility studies prior to a joint venture agreement.

Further assistance and advice can be obtained from various sources such as the Commercial section of the United Kingdom Permanent Representation (UKRep) office in Brussels, which exists to assist British companies to understand and participate in the programmes

2

administered by the European Institutions in Brussels. EMIC in London can also help and in recent years a Development Business Team in the Export Promotion Directorate can assist small and medium sized enterprises (SMEs) win business connected with aid funded projects. The Arab British Chamber of Commerce in London can also offer advice on the maze called 'Brussels'. Registration with Brussels for consultants is essential. Manufacturers with specialised products should also get pre-qualified to participate in EU funded projects

US

The US State Department and the Department of Commerce provide a wide range of information to US companies or representatives of US companies operating in Saudi Arabia.

The **Country Commercial Guide**, obtained for a fee from the US State Department, offers a comprehensive look at the business environment. This is naturally biased towards US business but much of the information is more generally applicable. US Exporters should contact STAT-USA at 1-800-STAT-USA for more information. The Country Commercial Guides can be downloaded from the Internet at: www. stat-usa.gov, www.state.gov and [www.mac.doc.gov], or can also be ordered as hard copy or on diskette from the National Technical Information Service (NTIS) at 1-800-553-NTS

The US Department of Commerce oversees a number of Export Assistance Centres across the US. These are noted in Appendix 3 and should be the starting point for US companies looking for specific export advice.

US Dept of Commerce
Trade Information Center
❏ Tel: +1 800-USA-TRADE Fax: +1 202 482-4473

Potential exporters should note that Saudi Arabia has decided to adopt ISO 9,000 as the approved standards for Saudi Arabia and SASO (The Saudi Arabian Standards Organisation) acts as the accreditation body. SASO has over 1,500 SASO and 1,000 Gulf promulgated standards and is actively pursuing hundreds more in various stages of development. The US has assigned a representative to SASO, from the US Department of Commerce's National Institute of Standards and

Technology (NIST) to advise the Saudi Government on developing standards. The US representative in Saudi Arabia may be contacted by fax on +966 1 488 3237.

For clarification on regulated product guidelines and procedures contact:

SASO Program Manager's Regional Office
❏ Tel: 1-713-475-9184 Fax: 1-713-475-2083

Australia

The Australian Trade Commission or Austrade is the federal governments export and investment facilitation agency. Austrade provides advice to Australian companies on general export issues, assistance in determining which overseas markets hold potential for their products and aid in building a presence in the market. First contact is usually through the Export Hotline telephone number (13 28 78). Through their network of global offices, including one in Riyadh, Austrade can assist with finding potential business partners or agents, prepare publicity material, organise product launches and offer assistance with attending suitable exhibitions. If Austrade cannot help with your specific requirement, they will direct you to an appropriate government or private service which can.

Austrade

Austrade Online is an enhanced website facility at www.austrade.gov.au which provides up to date reference points regarding international trade issues and export programmes. Australian companies can also take out a free of charge listing within the website allowing inclusion on a searchable database of products and services.

Austrade Online

Under their **Export Market Development Grant** (EMDG) scheme, Austrade may be able to reimburse eligible businesses for part of the export marketing costs they incur.

Austrade's Riyadh Office is located in the Diplomatic Quarter and may be contacted on:

❏ Tel +966 1 488 7788 Fax: +966 1 488 7458

Further Sources of Information

This is not a definitive list of bodies and merely indicates the types of organisations that exist and how they might help.

2

The Middle East Association

The Middle East Association is an independent private organisation set up in 1961 by a number of British companies to promote trade between the UK and the Middle East. It is a non-political and non-profit making organisation financed entirely by private subscription. It works with Middle Eastern Embassies in London and with other official and semi-official bodies such as the FCO, Trade Partners UK, the ECGD, COMET and the Confederation of British Industry (CBI). It also liaises with other trade associations and various Chambers of Commerce and Industry in the UK and overseas. The aim of the Association is to offer its members advice on all aspects of Middle East trade and to channel to them towards business opportunities, introductions and enquiries from overseas. The Association has a library and information centre at its offices in Bury Street – offices it shares with the COMET. With the support of Trade Partners UK it sponsors overseas missions and UK participation in trade exhibitions in the Middle East. The Association holds regular functions at its headquarters for its members, which include lunches with guest speakers from the Middle East. A fortnightly information digest is circulated to its members.

Middle East Association
Bury House
33 Bury Street, St James's
London SW1Y 6AX
❑ Tel:+44 20 7839 2137 Fax: +44 20 7839 6121
Website: www.the-mea.co.uk
Email: mail@the-mea.demon.co.uk

The Arab British Chamber of Commerce

The Arab British Chamber of Commerce (ABCC) was set up in 1975 and represents all the Arab Chambers of Commerce and the main UK Chambers. The ABCC is responsible for mutual trade and economic interests through meetings, exhibitions and publications throughout Middle East. A regular journal is freely available to those interested. The ABCC is also a facilitator for the European Community Investment Partners Scheme (ECIP) and has details of how to access the programme, together with details of many of the other EU funding programmes.

Arab British Chamber of Commerce
6 Belgrave Square
London SW1X 8PH
❑ Tel: +44 20 7235 4363 Fax: +44 20 7245 6688
Email: bims@abccbims.force9.co.uk

Chambers of Commerce or any trade or professional body
that you belong to may be able to provide information on
Saudi. They may not produce the material themselves but
as a member you may have access to their library where
such information is held. These bodies may also offer the
facility of conducting research on your behalf for a fee.
This is a more costly method but could well be time-
saving. You will have to be very specific in defining your
research project to obtain the maximum benefit.

Business Groups

The Kingdom has an active expatriate business community.
In each of the three main regions (Western, Central &
Eastern) there are associations of UK businessmen who
may be able to assist potential UK exporters with practical
and current advice regarding a particular market, product
or sector. Initial contact with these groups is best tracked
down via The British Embassy, Consulate or Trade Office
who will have current information regarding telephone
and fax numbers. Further information may also be
obtained at [www.rgbb.com]. There are also associations
of US businessmen who meet regularly to discuss matters
of mutual interest. They tend to be cautious when
promoting their activities and contact once again should
initially be made through the US Embassy.

Other publications

The British Embassy in Saudi Arabia publishes an annual
Saudi/British Trade Directory that identifies which Saudi
companies represent which British companies in the
Kingdom. They also produce a quarterly magazine
Enterprise UK which carries up to date contact
information and sector responsibilities of Saudi based
Embassy staff. Copies of publications are available in
Saudi Arabia from the British Embassy free of charge.
Both publications are compiled by Mead Management
Services Ltd. (MMSL) in the UK who will mail you
current copies for a small charge. Contact MMSL by fax:
+44 1249 460 602 or by email: amead@compuserve.com.

2

The Internet

Saudi Arabia's recent attachment to the world-wide-web has spawned a number of interesting sites, not all of which contain current, up-to-date or accurate material. Do try and check the credentials of information providers with officials before placing any reliance on material discovered when surfing.

One comprehensive site is the **US Library of Congress Study** on: www.lcweb2.loc.gov/frd/cs/satoc.html. This site covers an extraordainary number of topics concerning Saudi Arabia but much of the information is dated 1992 or earlier.

A more recent site at www.arab.net/saudi contains material dated 1996 but the best of the bunch for general background information is currently www.saudinf.com

Economic and Country Guides

Once you have gained an overview of the market in Saudi, you may want more detailed economic information or wish to concentrate on your particular sector. This is where the cost of research starts to increase. Armed with detailed information, the risk of unpleasant surprises later on will be much reduced. You will also be aware of the trends and the possible effects on your business and therefore able to plan for them.

The two best sources of detailed economic information and analysis are **Dun & Bradstreet** (D&B) and the **Economist Intelligence Unit** (EIU). D&B produce a Country Report on Saudi Arabia, which is available either in hardcopy or on CD-ROM and is updated every six months. It provides detailed analysis of the Saudi economy including political factors, short- and long-term issues and information on the trading and investing environments. D&B also produce two other publications helpful to exporters. The first is *The Exporters' Encyclopaedia* – an annual publication that provides information and advice on exporting to almost every country in the world. The second is the *International Risk and Payment Review* – a monthly publication that allows companies to keep up to date on issues affecting the trading environment in Saudi Arabia.

D&B can be contacted at:
Holmer's Farm Way
High Wycombe
Bucks HP12 4UL

2

❏ Tel: +44 1494 422000 Fax: +44 1494 422260
Website: www.dunandbrad.co.uk

The Economist Intelligence Unit produces a range of quarterly and annual publications, which provide detailed political and economic analysis of Saudi Arabia. The most useful of these publications is the quarterly Country Forecast, which includes a detailed five-year outlook. The EIU's Country Profile provides an annual overview of the country and Country Report provides a quarterly update on the market. Their on-line service Viewswire is a useful tool for monitoring developments in Saudi and other countries. The EIU also produces reports on the automotive, healthcare, telecommunications and financial sectors.

The **EIU** can be contacted at:
15 Regent Street
London, SW1Y 4LR
❏ Tel: +44 20 7830 1000 Fax: +44 20 7830 1023
Website: www.eiu.com Email: london@eiu.com

Or

The Economist Building
111 West 57th Street
New York, NY 10019, USA
❏ Tel: +1 212 554 0600 Fax: +1 212 586 1181

Another valuable source of information is **MEED** (Middle East Economic Digest) who publish a number of country reports and financial profiles, including the Middle East Business Finance Directory of the top 500 companies in the region.

MEED
21 John Street
London WC1N 2BP
❏ Tel: +44 20 7505 8000 Fax: +44 20 7831 9537
Website: www.meed.com

Banks, particularly the larger institutions that operate across the globe, may also be a useful source of information. The Saudi British Bank, part of the HSBC group, publishes a number of economic bulletins and a series of guides to business procedures in Saudi Arabia. These may be viewed on the bank's website: www.sabb.com.sa or obtained in the UK from:

MEED

2

The Saudi British Bank
18c Curzon Street
London
❏ Tel: +44 20 7629 3709 Fax: +44 20 7629 5872

Trade Associations

Also worth bearing in mind are the trade associations –
there is one for almost every conceivable industry. Some
of these are large and can be very active in promoting
exports. These organisations will assist their members to
take part in trade fairs, can organise seminars and
conferences to run concurrently with these events and
may target particular countries where they believe the
greatest opportunities exist for their members.

Full lists of all the associations in the UK are available
from CBD Research Ltd in Kent, who publish a directory
in hard copy or in CD-ROM format – full details at
www.glen.co.uk. Further information is also available
from Trade Partners UK.

Seminars and conferences are a good place to meet others
associated with Saudi Arabia or with a particular
industry. The content of the presentations at such
gatherings and the opportunities for networking during
the intervals are both important. The Middle East
Association holds a monthly 'at home' where members
meet and discuss the different issues and opportunities in
the area, including Saudi Arabia.

Travel Advice

The most convenient source of travel advice from the UK
is the Foreign and Commonwealth Office (FCO) travel
advisory service. This can be accessed for free either by
telephone or on-line. It provides succinct information and
advice on natural disasters, health concerns, security and
political issues. It is more than adequate for most
business travellers' needs. Be aware though that it is
aimed at a wide audience and is not geared solely
towards the business visitor's requirements. The
information may also be subject to political bias; negative
comments on a country can have an adverse impact on
the UK's relations with that country and therefore tend to
be avoided.

The FCO travel advisory service can be contacted on:

❏ Tel: +44 20 7238 4503/4
Website: www.fco.gov.uk/travel
or on Ceefax on BBC2 page 470

The US State department advice service can be found at:
www.state.gov/travel_warnings.html. Their reports can
sometimes seem alarmist as the US State Department is
legally obliged to publish any threats to US citizens and
their property of which it is aware. Also see
www.usis.egnet.net.

For travel information and advice geared specifically
towards the business traveller's needs, you must turn to
the private sector. Here there are some good but
expensive services that provide more frequently updated
reports than the FCO or State Department travel notices.
These services tend to be more forward-looking,
commenting for instance on the likelihood of further
security incidents or the possible deterioration or
improvement in the travel environment. They are also
usually more frank about a country as they do not
operate under the the political restrictions of the FCO or
State Department.

FCO

More Specialised Information

Although you have thoroughly researched the Kingdom,
your need for information, analysis and advice may not
be over. You may require detailed information on
prospective partners or analysis geared towards your
specific project or the business environment that you are
entering. Detailed investigation and analysis tailored to
particular specifications costs money. This course is
really only viable for companies involved in large
projects or where there is a lot at stake. It is also
advisable for companies considering a modest investment
at first but with the intention of making a long-term
commitment to Saudi Arabia.

The companies mentioned below – Control Risks, Kroll
Associates and Pinkertons – all provide tailor-made
confidential assessments of the business environment in
which you will operate in Saudi Arabia and provide
detailed information on the people and companies with
which you might form strategic partnerships. Some 'off

2

the shelf' material may be available, however the likelihood is that you will need to negotiate a fee based report tailored to the complexity of the information you require.

Control Risks Group
83 Victoria Street
London
SW1H 0HW
❏ Tel:+44 20 7222 1552 Fax: +44 20 7222 2296
Website: www.crg.com

Kroll Associates
25 Savile Row
London
W1X 0AL
❏ Tel: +44 20 7396 0000 Fax: +44 20 7969 2631
Website: www.krollworldwide.com

Pinkertons
Ferrari House
102 College Road
Harrow
Middx HA1 1ES
❏ Tel: +44 20 8424 8884 Fax: +44 20 8424 9744
Email: jbpcisuk@aol.com
Website: www.pinkertons.com

More focused reporting or feasibility studies relating to a particular product or market may be provided by management consultants with experience on the territory. These include:

ASA Consulting
PO Box 238 The Ridings
Cobham
Surrey KT11 2WP
❏ Tel: 01372 844 317 Fax: 01372 844 437
Email: asaconsult@btinternet.com

Maxima Group plc
29 Queen's Anne Gate
London SW1H 9BU
❏ Tel: +44 20 7227 3300 Fax: +44 20 7227 3311
Email: admin@maximag.co.uk
Website: www.maximag.co.uk

Keeping Up to Date

2

After you have thoroughly researched the Saudi market and started operations in the country, it is essential to keep up to date about developments both in your particular sector and in the wider market.

One method of accomplishing this is to monitor the press and media for stories on Saudi Arabia. The Internet editions of some newspapers and media organisations offer news email services, which can send you stories on specified subjects to your email address. Others allow you to produce customised pages, which are updated with stories on your chosen subjects. One of the best is CNN's service see cnn.com.

For a local perspective, the English-language newspapers include *The Arab News, The Saudi Gazette* and *Riyadh Daily*. Both local and international news articles in these papers provide an overview of current events. Do not assume however that the international press get things right. Articles may have been written by an uninformed reporter who has limited 'on the ground' experience or who may be following his own bias.

Very often the best contact will be with companies or individuals based in the Kingdom. In addition to the media, there is an extensive grapevine amongst the local and expatriate communities. The best thing to do is to get 'on the ground' yourself.

3

getting to Saudi Arabia

Getting to Saudi Arabia

The various considerations when arranging travel to Saudi Arabia.

Getting There

All visitors to Saudi Arabia require a visa and, with the exception of nationals from GCC (Gulf Corporation Council) states, they must be obtained in advance of travel. The requirements for Business Visas differ according to nationality, and it is important to note that visa requirements are liable to change at short notice. For up-to-date information contact the Saudi Arabian Embassy or Consulate to which you will apply. Applications are normally only accepted in the applicant's country of residence. At the time of writing, the Saudi Arabian Embassies in London and Washington only accept applications for Hajj or Umrah Visas through authorised travel agents. If an applicant is visiting the US and has been there legally for more than two months, an application may be made through an authorised agent. As a general rule, apply to the Saudi Arabian Embassy in your own capital. Contact details for Embassies in the UK, US, Australia and Canada are listed at the front of Annex One.

3

Visas

Different requirements exist for business visas and Hajj or pilgrimage visas. Briefly, a Hajj visa is one issued to a Muslim wishing to take part in the Hajj, which occurs during the first half of the twelfth Islamic month. Hajj visas are issued according to a quota system and it can be difficult to obtain one outside one's home country. An *Umrah* visa is issued to any Muslim who wishes to visit and pray in the Holy Cities of Makkah and Madinah, and is issued at any time other than the Hajj. The application must normally be made in one's home country or in the country in which one holds permanent residence. If the applicant is not from a Muslim country or does not have a Muslim name, he will be asked to provide an official document listing Islam as his religion. Converts must provide documentary evidence of their conversion from a mosque. An *Umrah* visa is valid for a week and allows only travel to Jeddah, Makkah and Madinah and the roads linking them. If travel is to be entirely by road, the visa covers travel from the border entry to the Holy Cities. Female travellers usually need to travel with their *mahram* – technically a guardian and usually restricted to father, husband or son. Written proof of the relationship must be provided. If the proposed accompanying guardian is not a relative (is, for example, a tour operator) then the *mahram*

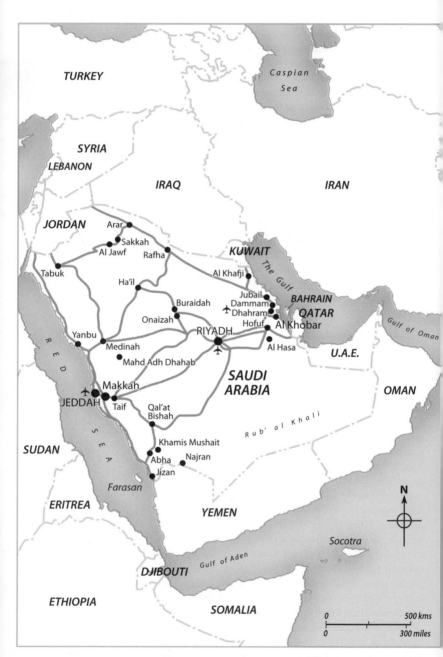

The Kingdom of Saudi Arabia

will be asked to provide a letter stating that he has no objection to the travelling companion. The Saudi Arabian Embassy in London has a website, www.saudiembassy.org.uk, with detailed information on this subject, as does the US website at www.saudiembassy.net.

At the time of writing it is possible to make a personal application for a Business Visa without using the services of a visa agent. This has not always been the case and readers should establish what rules apply at the time of application. The Saudi Arabian Embassy websites in the UK and US give full instructions on how to apply and what documentation should be provided. Readers in the UK should note that it is currently necessary to register on-line to obtain a registration number that must be presented when making an application in person or through an agency. Authorised Business Visa agencies differ from those who handle Hajj or *Umrah* Visas. Saudi Arabian Embassy websites around the world carry lists of Approved Visa Agents in various countries. One such company that has given the writer many years of good service in the UK is the Visa & Passport Service in St Stephens Mews in London. Contact them on Tel: +44 (0)20 7229 4784.

If you are going to live and work in Saudi Arabia, there is a great deal of paperwork (and bureaucratic red-tape) which your sponsor will have to complete on your behalf. You must provide copies of your employment contract and academic or professional qualifications, and undergo a comprehensive medical examination, for which the Embassy provides forms. An important part of the medical examination is a blood test showing that you are HIV negative (an AIDS test). Once you and your sponsor have completed the paperwork, which usually takes about six weeks, you will be informed of your visa number, which will entitle you to collect a visa. After arrival in the Kingdom, your visa will be converted to a residence visa and, in almost every case, you will at this point surrender your passport to your sponsor and be given an *igama*, or residence permit, which you should carry with you at all times. When leaving the country on holiday, your sponsor must obtain an

3

exit/re-entry visa for you and, upon your surrendering your *igama* to him, you will be given back your passport. Indeed, you will not be allowed to leave the country without an exit/re-entry visa stamp. If you are leaving and not returning, you will be issued an exit-only visa.

Unlike other countries of the GCC (Kuwait, Qatar, Bahrain, the United Arab Emirates and the Sultanate of Oman), Saudi Arabia has not previously issued Tourist Visas nor has it been possible for a hotel to sponsor a visitor. Saudi Arabia does not ban tourism; it is merely taking time to prepare for it.

Many commentators have suggested that the Kingdom has not been a popular destination for non-Muslim tourists, since there is little in the way of what might be regarded as tourist entertainment. They are wrong. There may not be alcohol-fuelled nightclubs in the cities, but there are huge numbers of cafés and restaurants, and shops galore! Yes, there is a lot of sand, but also dramatic mountains and valleys and a tremendous amount of fascinating places to visit.

In 1999 the Supreme Commission for Tourism was established. The Saudi government has accepted that tourism could be a key component in the national economy and in promoting the image of Saudi Arabia worldwide. A vast amount of work has already been done to prepare the Kingdom for an influx of tourists and a new Tourist Visa scheme was launched at the end of 2006.

The first steps towards welcoming tourists have been taken by Saudia, the national airline. Log on to the website at www.saudiairlines.com and be directed to the 'Discover Saudi Arabia' pages. Specific packages have been designed to showcase the country and links to approved international tour operators can be found. In mid 2006, the Director General of the Supreme Commission for Tourism, Prince Sultan bin Salman bin Abdul Aziz announced at a tourism exhibition in Dubai that 18 international tour operators had been approved to handle an initial 50,000 non-religious tourists per year; a number expected to rise to about 200,000 by 2010.

3

For more information in the UK contact:

Bales Tours
❏ Tel: +44 1306 732700 Fax: +44 1306 876 904
Email: enquiries@balesworldwide.com

In the US contact:
Peter Voll Associates in Palo Alto
❏ Tel: +1 650 812-7355 ext. 15 Fax: +1 650 812-7357.

As to the requirements for a Business Visa, up to date details are best obtained direct from the Embassy or Consulate where you intend to make your application. An outline of the requirements is as follows:

Business Visa

There are two types of Business Visa currently available; single entry and multiple entry. Up to date details are best obtained direct from the Embassy or Consulate where you intend to make your application. An outline of the requirements is as follows:

For a Single Entry Visa

● **1 The passport** should be valid for at least 6 months beyond the estimated period of stay in the Kingdom and have at least two empty adjacent pages to allow room for stamping. Jews are prohibited to enter and passports with Israeli stamps in them are likely to be refused. A new passport (without such a stamp) is normally available at consulates of Western countries.

● **2 A completed Business Visa Application form**. Forms may be downloaded from the Saudi Embassy websites as previously detailed. Forms may also be obtained in person or by writing to the Saudi Embassy and enclosing a stamped self-addressed envelope for its return. In addition to the personal information requested, applicants will need to give contact details for the Saudi company being visited who will need to action the third part of the requirement. In answer to the question 'Duration of stay in Saudi Arabia?' applicants should note that one month is the usual maximum period granted (see note below regarding extensions).

● **3 A letter of invitation from the Saudi host company.** certified by a Saudi Chamber of Commerce. No Chamber of Commerce certification is needed, however, for invitations issued by a government owned company,

3

such as Saudi Aramco, SABIC, Saudi Arabian Airlines, Ma'aden, or the Saudi Arabian General Investment Authority (SAGIA).

● **4 Two passport-sized photographs should be affixed to the application form.** The image must be taken against a white background and must be a full-face photograph. Side views are not accepted. Note: although the website information states that one photograph is sufficient, in practice, two are required.

● **5 The appropriate fee should be included.** A visa fee of £39.00 per passport is payable in the UK for all applicants. In the US the rates vary. For US citizens the fee is $108 for both single and multiple applications. For non-US citizens the fee is $54 for a single visa and $135 for a multiple. Applicants applying by post may pay by Postal Order or Bankers Draft to the order of the Saudi Embassy. Cash, personal or company cheques are NOT accepted with postal applications. Applicants from the Republic of Ireland should enclose a Bankers Draft ONLY. Personal callers to the Embassy may pay in cash or by personal cheque with a banker's card.

In the UK, applications may be lodged at the visa section between 9:00 am and 11:30 am Monday to Friday inclusive. Personal callers will be given a date-stamped numbered ticket, to be presented on collection. A minimum of 24 hours is required to process visas.

Staff will inform you when the passport will be ready for collection. Postal applications or personal callers unable to return to the Embassy at the due time should include a prepaid special delivery envelope with their application form. Return may take 4-5 days after lodging.

Visa validity starts from the date of issue and is normally limited to one month. This means that your visit must commence within one month of the date stamp on the visa. The date stamp is based on the Gregorian calendar.

The period of stay begins upon arrival in Saudi Arabia. However, applicants should note that all government business in Saudi Arabia is conducted according to the Islamic hijra calendar. The Gregorian date on documents is there for your convenience only and is in no way to be construed as official. The official date will be the Islamic one, and as the Islamic year is 11 days shorter than the Gregorian, confusion can, and often does, result. For example, a visa showing a period of stay as one month is valid for an Islamic month, not a Gregorian one. If the visitor stays for a Gregorian month, there is a distinct possibility he will have overstayed his visa by a day or two and he will almost surely encounter difficulties with the authorities when he attempts to leave the Kingdom.

Should a visitor need to extend his stay in the Kingdom, even by one day, his sponsor will need to apply for an extension to the visa. This is best done at least three days before the initial period ends and not be left until the period has expired.

Multiple Entry Visa

The requirements for a multiple entry visa are as above, but the sponsor's invitation letter must specifically request multiple entry. A multiple entry visa will normally be valid for a maximum of six months but will still be limited to a maximum of one month per visit. It is not currently possible to gain an extension to a visit under a multiple entry visa.

The fee for a multiple entry visa is £96 in the UK; in the US it is $108 for US citizens and $135 for non-US citizens.

In the US the sponsor will need to provide an explanation of why multiple visits are required. This will be reviewed by the Consul before deciding whether or not to grant multiple entry.

Those in Saudi Arabia on Business Visas do not need an exit visa to leave the country. However, the single-entry condition is strict and once you have left you cannot return without a new visa. Visitors to the Eastern Province are often invited to visit Bahrain, perhaps for an evening dinner or for a relaxing weekend. The stories are legion of visitors who thought they could pop across the Causeway and come back again, provided they did it within their 'month' visa, to discover to their cost that the Saudi authorities refused them re-entry.

Female Travellers

It can be difficult, but not impossible, for a single woman to get a visa. Officially unaccompanied women must either travel with or be met at the airport by their sponsor or husband and have confirmed onward reservations as far as their final destination in Saudi

Arabia. If met by a sponsor, it is worth noting that there are restrictions on women travelling by car with men who are not related by blood or marriage: enquiries can be made at the Information Centre or Embassy. Applications from women over 40 are more likely to be granted than those for younger women.

In theory, a single businesswoman may be granted a visa provided the company inviting her has obtained approval from the Ministry of Foreign Affairs first. In practice, this process may take several weeks and many businesswomen find that travelling with a Trade Mission can ease their passage. In the UK the Middle East Association can assist.

Other Visas

In addition to the Hajj, *Umrah*, Business (Visitor), and Residence visa there are three other types of visa.

Airport Transit Visas

There are Transit Visas for people passing through Saudi airports. These are issued only after you have satisfied the Saudi Embassy that you had absolutely no choice but a transit stop in the Kingdom. You will have to surrender your passport to the immigration authorities at the airport and collect it on your way out. The Transit Visa is normally limited to 24 hours, although some instances of 72 hour passes have been reported. In theory, transits of less than 18 hours do not need a visa, but it is unlikely you will be allowed to leave the airport. When making an application for a Transit Visa, keep in mind that your passport must already include any visa for the destination country. According to the Washington website, ladies cannot apply for Transit Visas if not accompanied by a male relative. Transit Visas are free of charge.

Road Transit Visas

These are relatively straightforward. People driving between Jordan and either Yemen or Kuwait are normally given three-day transit visas. These are usually issued only by the Saudi Embassies in Amman or Sana'a. You are required to go to the Embassy with your passport containing a visa for the country at the other end of the trip. People driving between Bahrain, Qatar or the UAE and Jordan may be given seven-day Transit Visas. Those driving between Oman and Jordan are required to get the Transit Visa in Abu Dhabi. It is worth repeating that women are not permitted to drive in Saudi Arabia.

Student Visa

Applications for Student Visas must be accompanied by a reference note showing the number and date of the Student Visa issued by the Ministry of Foreign Affairs or its branches in Jeddah or Dammam.

Additional requirements are: the applicant's original Birth Certificate plus a copy; original High School Diploma and a copy (if applying in the US) and a recent police report with details of any criminal record.

Bear in mind that much of the above may be subject to change at short notice, and the whim of the official on duty can affect the interpretation of the rules. There are many tales of individuals who obtain visas in their country of origin only to find them invalid at the Saudi border, or who arrive at the Saudi border having been instructed by their local Saudi Embassy that the border is the appropriate place to obtain a Transit Visa, to be told that only an Embassy can issue one. The basic rule is to double-check all your facts with your local Saudi Embassy and, if possible, with the authorities in Saudi Arabia before commencing travel.

Flights

In 2003 the airline industry was stunned by the British Airways decision to suspend flights both to and from the Kingdom temporarily following increased terrorist activity in the region. In 2005 the airline ceased flying to Saudi Arabia on commercial grounds, claiming the war in the region was deterring both business and leisure travel. Several commentators claimed that the decision was actually made because of the difficulties in getting flight crews to agree to fly the route.

Britain's second largest carrier, bmi, stepped into the breech and by the middle of 2006 was flying at least three times a week into both Jeddah and Riyadh. Most of the other major European carriers also fly to both destinations. bmi fly out of Heathrow Terminal One making it convenient for passengers arriving in London from other domestic airports. Flight time from the UK to either destination is about 6 ½ hours.

3

The Eastern Province is not as well served by the international carriers. Many airlines fly to nearby Bahrain more frequently and if the Eastern Province is your destination, it is easy to land in Bahrain and take the short drive across the Causeway linking Bahrain with the mainland.

Another popular choice for travellers from Europe and the US is to enter the Kingdom via Doha, Dubai or Abu Dhabi. Although this can add significantly to the flight time, some carriers offer free overnight accommodation in those cities, allowing for a little extra sight-seeing or shopping.

Ticket prices vary tremendously and it is worth shopping around. Even during peak travel times, it is possible to pay less than £400 for the same economy seat for which others can pay more than £1,300. Worth keeping in mind is that different airlines employ different cabin configurations with more than one class of service and special offers with some restrictions may be available for less than the published fares.

Membership of many of the Frequent Flyer programmes operated by most airlines is worth investigating for regular travellers. The Diamond Club scheme operated by bmi has worked extremely well for the writer, as has the scheme operated by Gulf Air whose Frequent Flyer miles are valid for 10 years.

On Arrival

Passengers not complying with Saudi conventions of dress and behaviour, including those who appear to be intoxicated, will be refused entry even if their passports/visas are in order. Islam, the official religion, encompasses all aspects of life and observance of any other religion is forbidden. Non-Muslim religious services are illegal and public display of non-Islamic religious articles such as crosses and bibles is not permitted. Such items will be confiscated on arrival. Travel to Makkah and Madinah, the cities where the two most holy mosques of Islam are located, is forbidden to non-Muslims. The importation and use of narcotics, alcohol and pork products is also forbidden. Penalties for importing drugs are severe and include the death penalty.

3

All international arrivals now have their luggage inspected. Whilst this is usually done by x-ray machine, occasionally passengers may be asked to open suitcases to allow a physical inspection.

Visitors arriving in the Kingdom by road, for example via the Bahrain causeway should expect to have all their belongings inspected. Vehicles may be stripped to make sure nothing illegal is being concealed.

Timing

While the more traditional businesses still work from Saturday to Wednesday with an option of Thursday morning as well, many operations, particularly those in the finance sector are switching to a Sunday to Thursday operation, with Friday and Saturday as days off. Keep in mind that since Saudi Arabia is three hours ahead of GMT it can take a little time to adjust after a long haul flight.

Trade Missions

Getting to Saudi Arabia is not a particularly simple operation for a company without contacts. Arranging for a suitable invitation is often the major stumbling block. Companies wanting to investigate the market might consider joining one of the special trade missions that regularly visit the Kingdom. These are often arranged by UK Chambers of Commerce and may attract some funding from the UKTI or other government administrations.

Potential 'missionaries' may be able to join all or part of a trip involving the Kingdom and have their visas, flights, accommodation, etc. arranged. The Middle East Association in London is probably best placed to handle enquires on what missions are planned and when. Many of their missions are subsidised by the British Offset Office who encourage Saudi-British business as part of the Al Yamana arrangements. Contact them on
❏ Tel: +44 (0)20 7839 2137 Fax +44 (0)20 7839 6121

Health and Insurance

Recommendations regarding vaccinations vary from time to time and your local GP should have current details. Hepatitis A, polio & typhoid inoculations should be

3

considered as well as malaria tablets. Depending on which part of the Kingdom you are visiting and which other countries are included in your tour, you may need yellow fever and meningitis protection. If come from a country where yellow fever is endemic, you will need to show a vaccination certificate on arrival. Seek advice well in advance of your proposed travel dates since many of the innoculations may not be effective until several weeks after treatment.

Visitors should be aware that there have been cases of cerebral malaria, some fatal, in the Jizan area of southwest Saudi Arabia. The outbreak was local and did not affect Jeddah or other areas of Saudi Arabia. Visitors intending to travel to the Jizan area should seek up-to-date medical advice before travelling.

Despite the above, there are rarely any unusual health risks and normal precautions apply. For example, as some of the water is untreated and is not safe to drink, use bottled water whenever possible. Care should be exercised with some dairy products, which may not be pasteurised. Fruit and vegetables should be peeled before consumption.

Saudi Arabia is usually covered under standard worldwide travel insurance policies available from reputable insurance companies or brokers. An annual premium is likely to cost from £100 – £200. No other special insurance arrangements are recommended.

British and US nationals travelling to Saudi Arabia should remain alert to developments in the Middle East. Any increase in regional tension can affect travel advice. Both British and US authorities acknowledge that Saudi Arabia is one of a number of countries where British/US interests are vulnerable to terrorism.

Jeddah Islamic Seaport

the ground rules

4

the ground rules

This section takes the reader by the hand and talks through the nitty-gritty of everyday life, from how to get aaround to how much to tip the bell-boy. Knowledge of these essentials provides the confidence to go out and do business effectively.

Currency

For over 20 years, since devaluation in 1986, the official exchange rate has been pegged at 3.745 Saudi Riyals to the US dollar. The Saudi Riyal is usually abbreviated to SR but occasionally SAR is used. Banking transactions use rates close to the official rate. In the spring of 2006, as the dollar declined, neighbouring Kuwait revalued its exchange rate, fuelling speculation that the Saudi Riyal might follow suit, but this has yet to happen.

Notes are issued in units of SR1, 10, 20, 50, 100, 200 and 500. The Riyal is divided into 100 hallalahs, and coins are issued in units of 10, 25, 50 and 100 (SR1).

Sterling rates fluctuate daily and over the last five years have averaged SR6.36 / £1. The spread though has been vast varying from a low of SR5.28 and a high of SR7.29. The Saudi Arabian Monetary Agency (SAMA) has intervened at times to keep the exchange rate pegged to the dollar.

Banking

The Saudi Arabian Monetary Agency, founded in 1952, is the Saudi central bank. Its charter is to regulate and control the Saudi banking sector, issue currency, support the Riyal at home and abroad and generally to encourage and develop the Kingdom's banking sector. Financing is available to Saudi and non-Saudi businesses.

Commercial banking has undergone tremendous growth during the course of the country's development. The rapid expansion of deposits has allowed the banking system to take on a leading role in marshalling Saudi financial resources to fund the expanding activities of the private sector.

As for the stock market, which has existed informally since 1954, the Capital Markets Law of June 2003 established the Saudi Arabian Stock Exchange (SASE) as a private sector entity. By then, market capitalization stood at over US$ 127 billion, confirming Saudi Arabia as the largest market in the region and one of the largest emerging markets in the world, although the number of companies listed remained comparatively low at 65.

Only residents of the Kingdom are allowed to maintain bank accounts, Business visitors, no matter how frequent

4

Money

4

their visits, may not open accounts. Most major international credit and debit cards will work in the ATMs and are usually accepted in stores and hotels.

The main commercial banks operating in Saudi Arabia are as follows:

The National Commercial Bank, originally formed in 1938 but changed to its current name in 1954. In 1999, the Saudi government, through the Ministry of Finance's Public Investment Fund, acquired a majority holding.

Riyad Bank was established in 1957. (100 per cent Saudi owned.)

Al-Rajhi Banking and Investment Corporation. Formerly a money changing company, Al-Rajhi was accorded banking status in 1988. (100 per cent Saudi owned.)

The Samba Financial Group (Saudi American Bank) was formed in 1980 to take over the operations of Citibank in Jeddah & Riyadh. In 1999 Samba merged with United Saudi Bank (USB). In 2003 the Bank moved to full local management and Citibank subsequently sold its remaining 20 per cent share capital to a Saudi agency.

SABB. Established in 1978 as The Saudi British Bank when it took over the operations of the British Bank of the Middle East, the name was changed to SABB in 2006 (40 per cent HSBC Holdings).

The Arab National Bank commenced business in 1980 when it took over the operations of Arab Bank Ltd in the Kingdom.

Banque Saudi Al Fransi (31 per cent Credit Agricole Indosuez).

Saudi Hollandi Bank claims the title of First Bank in the Kingdom having been established in 1926 as the Netherlands Trading Society.(40 per cent ABN Amro.)

Saudi Investment Bank (SAIB) was established in 1976. Shareholders include J.P. Morgan Chase and Mizuho Corporate Bank (formerly the Industrial Bank of Japan).

Bank Al-Jazira (5.8 per cent National Bank of Pakistan).

Al Bilad Bank, established as a joint stock company in 2004, was founded by a group of companies previously operating as investors and money changers.

4

The Saudi Arabian Capital Market Authority (CMA), the regulator of the stocks exchange and capital markets, has given its approval to HSBC and SABB to establish the first full-service, independent investment bank in the Kingdom of Saudi Arabia licensed under the new Capital Market Law.

HSBC, through a wholly-owned subsidiary, will hold 60 per cent of the equity in the new company and SABB, in which HSBC has a 40 per cent shareholding, will hold the remaining 40 per cent. The joint venture, known as **HSBC Saudi Arabia Limited**, is established as a limited liability company headquartered in Riyadh

Transport

Saudi Arabia's major cities are separated by long distances and while the main form of transport within cities is the car, travel between them is easier by air. Although many of the worlds' major airlines cover international routes to and from the Kingdom, the national carrier, Saudi Arabian Airlines, has been the only carrier allowed to operate internal flights.

The market is, however, changing and in December 2005 a new low cost airline called SAMA was announced. SAMA was founded by Investment Enterprises Ltd, chaired by HRH Prince Bandar bin Khalid al Faisal, with the support of Mango Aviation Partners, a UK firm specialising in low fare airline start-ups. Mango was established by a number of senior executives with many years experience in the UK and European budget airline industry. In 2006, on behalf of the shareholders, Mango are in the process of establishing the airline, subject to regulatory approval, and are extensively recruiting to carry the airline forward.

For many years there were only two types of tickets available, economy or first class. Economy tickets for flights within the Kingdom are very reasonably priced, On some routes on certain aircraft a business class alternative is now available.

In January 2000 an economy return trip from Riyadh to Jeddah cost SR540. In 2006 it was still only SR560. Business Class seats, where available, would be SR960. A first-class fare for the same route is SR1,500. A return trip from Riyadh to Dammam is SR300 for economy or SR650 in first. Ticket prices for the round trip Jeddah-Dammam-

Transport

Jeddah are SR780, SR1,370 or SR1,880. Flights are often over-subscribed since some passengers reserve several options, deciding only which flight to take when they get to the airport. If you are prepared to put up with an unseemly scrum and risk wasting your time, it is often possible to join the waiting list of an apparently full flight and get a seat at the last minute.

Driving is on the right and only men are permitted to drive. Car hire desks are located at all the major airports and major hotels. Car hire costs about SR100 per day, although cheaper rates can be arranged for longer periods. Copies of a valid driving licence and passport are required. In the event of an accident, a police certificate is required for insurance claims or repairs to the vehicle. Cars involved in accidents should be left wherever they come to rest and should not be moved until after the police are in attendance. Traffic hold-ups (which are frequent, particularly in the rush hour) are usually caused by such temporary blockages while drivers wait for police attention.

Driving in Saudi Arabia can be hazardous and, while there are heavy penalties for dangerous driving, accidents still occur. Road signs are frequently ignored, as are lane markings. Particular care should be taken at road junctions where it is not uncommon for a vehicle in the left-hand lane to turn right, or vice-versa. Overtaking is permitted on either side where space allows and it is legal to filter right at a road junction even if the lights are red. At some roundabouts it is best to give way to traffic already on the roundabout, at others you may have to give way to traffic joining the roundabout.

Even experienced drivers can get caught out. Take care, for example, if you hire a car from Riyadh airport, the slip road out of the car park emerges onto the fast lane of the airport highway!

The speed limit on motorways is usually 120kph, and in town 80kph. In an attempt to improve driving conditions a new set of penalties was imposed in 1999, which include on-the-spot fines for speeding and a day or two in jail for other offences. By 2006 these fines were being reported as one day in jail and SR600 fine for speeds between 140-159 kph, three days in jail and SR900 fine for speeds between 160-189kph; and seven days in jail and SR1500 fine for any speed above 190kph. In addition anyone caught speeding may have the vehicle confiscated for a period of at least five days. These penalties seem to have resulted in a rise in the use of radar-detectors, which are 'technically' illegal in the Kingdom but still seem to be available!

New visitors are recommended to take advantage of the widely available taxis, or, better still, the chauffeur-driven limousine services available from leading companies. All taxis are now required to have meters fitted; not all of them are used, and at times the calibration can seem erratic. It is advisable to agree a rate in advance and avoid a nasty shock at the journey's end. After rates have been agreed it is not necessary to add a tip.

Buses are in use, and fares are very cheap, however in the city these are limited to some dirty and scary mini-buses whose drivers ply their routes at a frantic pace. Inter-city coach services exist, with a fare from Riyadh to Jeddah of only SR135.

New arrivals will usually be met by their hosts, but most leading hotels have an airport collection service if requested in advance. A taxi from the airport to most hotels in the city should cost no more than SR60 and take about 30 minutes.

International businessmen should note that only Muslims are allowed to enter the Holy Cities of Makkah and Medinah. Passports are checked and there is no known legal way of circumventing this obstacle. Meetings with businessmen from these cities are best arranged at facilities in Jeddah.

Travellers between Riyadh and Dammam have the added option of using the train. The train may stop at Hofuf and Abqaiq and tickets are best bought the day before. The train takes about four hours. Tickets cost SR150 for a first class return and SR120 for second class. Two trains run in each direction on most days. A third type of ticket, Rehab Class, is offered at SR260 return.

Tel: +966 1 473 4444 ext 1 for reservations; ext 2 for departure schedules.

4

Contact:
Avis

❏ Riyadh (01) 476 1300
Jeddah: (02) 661 0925
Al Khobar: (03) 895 4702
Yanbu: (04) 322 7588
Jubail: (04) 346 6777

Budget Rent-a-Car

❏ Riyadh (01) 473 0739 Fax: 476 4405
Jeddah: (02) 669 3384/669 3632 Fax: 669 5833
Dammam: (03) 834 8901 Fax: 834 8611

Thrifty Car Rental

❏ Riyadh: (01) 478 4332
Jeddah: (02) 640 3470 Fax: 640 3813
Al Khobar: (03) 899 6600
Al Kharj: (012) 548 2819

Communications

Mail

There is no home delivery service available from the Post Office. All mail is delivered to Post Office boxes located at the major post offices. It is the responsibility of the box holder to check whether or not mail has arrived. Incoming mail can some times take weeks to reach the intended recipient. International outgoing mail can be unreliable and may take 5-10 days to reach Europe.

Couriers

Courier services are widely used both within and between cities in the Kingdom and internationally. A wide choice of carriers is available including DHL and Federal Express. Minimum charges apply, making it considerably more expensive than the postal service, but these services can be relied upon.

It is not uncommon for passengers on international flights leaving the Kingdom to take mail for friends or neighbours.

Dialing codes

The international dialling code for Saudi Arabia is +966 followed by an area code and the local number. A list of area codes is contained in the appendix. Dialling from city to city within the Kingdom requires use of the area code. Local calls within a city are virtually free, although some hotels may levy a minimum fee. Independently operated Call Cabins located in most areas allow local and international calling at significantly lower rates than in the hotels. Some Call Cabins also have a fax facility. STC (The Saudi Telephone Company) retains a monopoly on all land lines.

Extensive use is made within the Kingdom of mobile phones. Since Mobily became active in 2005, STC no longer has a monopoly. Mobily is the trade name of the first company to obtain a GSM licence after STC, and is owned by a consortium led by UAE Company Etisalet. Both STC and the Kingdom's second operator launched 3G services in 2006 and a third licence is expected to be granted in late 2006. 15 million phones were said to be in use in 2006 with the number forecast to rise to 22 million within three years.

Authorities in the Kingdom have not reacted favourably to new technology and mobile phones with built-in cameras were initially banned after many users were accused of spreading obscenity. That ban was overturned in 2004, but religious authorities continue to call for stronger laws prohibiting their use. One newspaper report in 2005 claimed that a proposal before the Shura Council should impose a 12-year sentence, a SR100,000 fine and 1,000 lashes for those circulating improper images through the phone!

The internet is available in Saudi Arabia and more and more companies are making use of e-mail. In 2006, 28 ISPs were registered, though not all of them appeared to be active. Users were estimated at approximately 2.5 million in 2006. Users of the STC service will find that their internet access is often restricted, since most of the internet traffic is fed through KACST (King Abdulaziz City for Science and Technology) who perform a censorship role. KACST claim that 95 per cent of the sites they block are pornographic, but they do admit that in such a conservative society, mistakes are sometimes made and sites might have been blocked in error. KACST handles the technology, but the decision on which sites to block is taken by the Communications and Information Technology Commission (CITC).

STC has come in for severe criticism since 1999 for failing to provide a good service and lagging behind the available technology. Many users have gone down the satellite route in order to get faster and cheaper service. The satellite routes usually bypass the KACST censorship, but even

4

Radio

those services have caused controversy and in 2003 the Council of Ministers called for the suspension of licences from satellite service providers. Various press releases in mid 2006, suggested that STC was investing heavily in new technology and would soon be able to offer a wide range of premium quality multimedia and high-speed data services.

English language radio stations are hard to find. Radio Riyadh puts out some programmes in English on 97.7 FM. More popular are the American Forces Radio stations which play a wide selection of more popular Western music – 107.9 FM in Riyadh and 103.9 FM in Jeddah. In the Eastern Province more Gulf-based stations can be picked up with decent equipment. Information on the frequencies for BBC World Service may be found on www.bbc.co.uk/worldservice.

Private radio and TV stations may not operate in Saudi Arabia but the country is a key target for pan-Arab satellite services. MBC and Orbit channels seem to be the most popular. There are four State television channels Saudi 1, Saudi 2, Arriyadiah and Al-Ekhbaria. Some of the channel 2 programs are in English. Most hotels operate satellite reception providing a range of light entertainment and news channels. The first phase of digital terrestrial television services (DTT) was rolled out in mid 2006 and is set to provide a service to 22 Saudi cities by February of 2007. The new service will include four radio stations and a new TV channel specifically designed for the Saudi market.

Public Holidays

Saudi Arabia works on the Hijra lunar calendar. Taking the date of the Prophet Muhammad's exodus from Makkah to Medinah as its starting point, it has 354 days in a year. The result is an annual Islamic date occurring eleven days earlier in each subsequent year of the Gregorian (solar) calendar. Over and above this, dates of festivals are dependent on the actual sighting of the moon, so during cloudy periods the dates may stray from the astronomers' predictions. The Islamic New Year will fall on Jan 20th 2007 and Jan 10th in 2008 but is not taken as a holiday. The two official holiday periods are Eid al Fitr and the Eid Al Ahda, the first being the breaking of the fast immediately after Ramadan and the latter the feast of sacrifice following the Hajj. In 2006-7 those dates are expected to start on Dec 31st 2006 for the

4

Eid Al Adha and October 13th for the Eid Al Fitr. Although these feast days are technically three days, the holiday usually stretches from 10 to 14 days.

Business visitors should take particular care to avoid these times since although only the government offices are closed for the entire holiday, much of the private sector chooses to take time off during these periods.

In 2005, King Abdullah declared that Saudi National Day would become a new public holiday. September 23rd is the date the Kingdom of Saudi Arabia was founded in 1932. When this falls on a Friday, the Saturday will be the holiday.

Ramadan

The holy month of Ramadan is a period first of fasting, then of celebration. Muslims will not eat, drink or smoke during daylight hours (particularly tough when Ramadan falls during the long summer days). As a non-Muslim visitor it is only courteous to do likewise when in public; it is usually possible, however, to be served in the privacy of your hotel room. Throughout Ramadan, working hours are severely curtailed and shop opening times become erratic, particularly towards the end of the month, opening for a few hours in the morning and then for extended periods at night after the fast has been broken. The period of fasting ends with Eid Al-Fitr, when everything shuts down for a few days.

Fasting

Ramadan

All of this can make it very difficult to conduct business effectively and although businesses continue to operate it is probably advisable to schedule your visit before or after Ramadan. In 2007 Ramadan begins on Sept 13th, in 2008 - Sept 2nd and in 2009 - Aug 22nd.

Working Days

Friday (*yawm al-juma'a*) is a day of rest and prayer. Thursday is also taken as a holiday, although most shops and offices will be open in the mornings until noon. The working week starts on Saturday morning, and runs through until Thursday lunchtime. Note however that some sectors are slipping into a Friday /Saturday weekend to allow more 'working-time' contact with the west.

Hours of Business

Business hours vary in different parts of the country and in different types of business. Many companies will

4

operate in two distinct shifts from 8 or 9 am until 12 noon or 1 pm, opening again from 3 or 4 pm until 6 or 7 pm. Actual hours may vary from day to day to fit in around the changing prayer times. Government offices usually work from 7.30 am until 2.30 pm from Saturday to Wednesday. Banks tend to operate from 8 am until the noon prayer and then again from about 4.30 pm until 8 pm. As a general comment, businesses in the Eastern Province tend to operate earlier hours than those in the Western Province. Many Western managed companies attempt to operate a 9-5 regime. No firm rule applies and it is best to check with each company as to their own practice.

Retail operations generally open from about 9 am until the noon prayer, remaining closed until about 4 pm when they reopen until late. Many supermarkets now operate round the clock, closing only at prayer times for about 30 minutes each time.

During Ramadan, the month of fasting, working hours are generally shortened by at least two hours. Opening hours may be significantly altered in their timing to fit local conditions.

Business Etiquette

Arabic is the official language, although English is widely used in business circles. Letters or faxes to official bodies such as Chambers of Commerce are supposed to be in Arabic.

Modern Saudi Arabia has adopted many of the business methods and styles of the West, but some differences remain. Most importantly business can be conducted only after a degree of trust and familiarity has been established. Considerable time may be spent exchanging courtesies, and several visits may be needed to secure business. Learn a little about the Kingdom and the people and avoid political or religious comment. Above all, do not appear to be impatient with unforeseen delays. In Saudi culture, bargaining is considered natural and to be enjoyed. Do not hurry or be hurried. Do not set yourself restrictive deadlines.

Dress

Men and women should dress conservatively. If attending a business meeting, Western style suits are the best choice. When dealing with the older generation of Saudis, it is best for men to wear long sleeved shirts. In Jeddah, which is rather more cosmopolitan than the rest of the country (it can also be very hot and humid), jackets are not as essential and short sleeved shirts are acceptable. Outside the office, men should not wear shorts or tank tops unless in the privacy of a housing compound or on the beach.

It is customary to shake hands at the beginning and end of business meetings and if you are seated when a visitor enters the room it is polite to stand. On the rare occasions females are present, a male visitor should not attempt to shake the lady's hand unless it is offered first. Business visitors should arrange their itineraries to allow for long meetings, as Saudis often maintain an 'open office' in which they will sign papers, take telephone calls, and converse with friends or colleagues who drop by. Although your host may not be, it is advisable to be punctual, but, do not be offended if you have to wait a while. Tea, soft drinks, and traditional Saudi coffee (*gahwa*) are usually offered. The coffee is strongly flavoured with cardamom and occasionally with cloves or saffron. *Gahwa* may be served from a traditional Arabic pot (*dallah*) or a thermos flask. It is poured into small handleless cups about the size of eggcups. The server will continue to fill the cup until the guest returns the cup to him. One to three cups should be taken for politeness, after which the cup should be wiggled between thumb and forefinger when returning it to the server to indicate that you have finished. Tea or *chai* is usually served very sweet in small glasses without milk.

Drinks

Many Saudi businessmen have been educated or have travelled extensively in the West and are sophisticated in dealing with Westerners. In many offices, the serving of *gahwa* is no longer the norm; instead the visitor will be offered a choice of – Turkish or American coffee or traditional English tea. Fresh pasteurised cow's milk is relatively new to Saudi Arabia and many companies will use long-life or powdered milk when making 'English' tea!

For the most part, travellers can rely on the usual Western manners and standards of politeness to see them through, with a few additional rules. A key point is to remember to use only the right hand when offering or accepting something. The left hand is traditionally used for taking care of personal hygiene.

It may be also be considered discourteous to ask about a man's wife or daughters; ask instead about his family. Do not attempt to get too personal too quickly – take the lead from your host and don't be too pushy.

4

An invitation to dinner may occasionally be offered to business visitors, especially if you are in Saudi Arabia to see someone specific. Dinner may be a Western meal at a restaurant or hotel, or occasionally a rather grander affair in which food is served Saudi-style. If you are invited to the home of a Saudi for a party or reception, a meal is normally served at the end of the evening, and guests will not linger after eating. Shoes are usually removed before entering a Saudi *majlis* (living room) – again take the lead from your host.

Dining out

If you are invited to a Saudi meal, you may be expected to sit on the floor and eat from the communal plate. This will usually be a large dish of rice topped with a half or a whole lamb, or chicken portions. Eat with the right hand and at all times avoid sitting with the soles of the feet pointed at another person. The custom is to take a small portion of rice with a little of the meat into your right hand and squeeze it into a ball, pushing the ball into your mouth with your thumb. This may require practice, but persevere if you can. The platters are often so large each diner has his own area of the plate but it is not unusual for one of the other diners to offer particularly choice morsels to the visitor. Customs and manners differ, so be observant and adapt your behaviour to that of your host.

The call to prayer

Saudi Arabia requires strict adherence to Islamic principles. Muslims are obliged to pray in the direction of the Holy City, Makkah, five times a day. The prayer times are published in the newspaper and occur at dawn, noon, afternoon, sunset, and evening. Stores and restaurants close for approximately half an hour at these times. The call to prayer is broadcast from every mosque and occasionally over the tannoy in shops and offices. It is quite common and perfectly acceptable for meetings to break up while worshippers leave the office to pray. Your host may leave the building and pray in a nearby mosque, he may join other colleagues and pray in a separate office, or he may simply take out his prayer mat and perform his duty in the same room. If staging promotional events or product demonstrations, anticipate these prayer-breaks and be prepared.

Islam and its principles are upheld in public life by the religious police (*Mutawa'a*), who circulate widely and are active in punishing misdemeanours (such as shopkeepers who conduct business during prayer time).

4

Although it is possible just to turn up at the British Embassy offices, business travellers seeking appointments with officials at the British Embassy in Riyadh should contact the Commercial Section in advance.
Tel: +966 1 488-0077 Fax +966 1 488-2373.

Business travellers to Saudi Arabia seeking appointments with officials at the US Embassy in Riyadh should contact the Commercial Section in advance.

Tel: +966 1 488-3800 ext. 1527 or 1516;
Fax: +966 1 488-3237

Women

More and more women are entering the workforce, and it is gradually becoming more acceptable for businesswomen to visit Saudi Arabia. There is still, however, strict gender separation in the Kingdom and special arrangements may have to be made for female visitors to meet male Saudi businessmen. The exception to the rule is in hospitals where male and female workers often work side by side.

Many offices and public buildings forbid females to enter even for a short visit, and business meetings may need to be scheduled in hotel lobby areas or separate buildings where appropriate security measures are in place. Ladies should check precise arrangements for attending exhibitions for example, since some 'officials' may prevent their access.

Restaurants are required to maintain separate sections for single men and 'families'. In some areas, unaccompanied women will be allowed into 'family' areas, in others unaccompanied women are refused entry.

Some shops are considered 'women only' areas where men will be refused entry even though the shop assistants may be male. More than one of these 'women only' facilities have been closed down by the religious authorities who felt that the gender separation rules might have been abused. Hotels may refuse to allow a single woman to take a room unless their sponsor has supplied an authorisation letter.

At the Kingdom Centre in Olaya, in Riyadh, one floor of the complex is a 'women only' shopping mall, which is

4

managed and staffed exclusively by women. Women are meant to remove their veils on entry so that security staff can see that they are not men in disguise!

When accompanying a husband on a business trip, wives may be excluded from social gatherings or may be entertained separately. On all occasions women are advised to wear loose-fitting and concealing clothing with long skirts, wrist-length sleeves, and modest necklines. Tight trousers or low-neck lines may be considered inappropriate. Whatever they wear in private, and there are some beautiful clothes in the shops, most women choose to wear the *abaya* in public. The *abaya* is a lightweight black cloak that completely covers what is worn underneath. Although it is not the law, it is sensible to follow this trend and avoid offense.

With the winds of change constantly battering the Kingdom, the 'problem' of dealing with the businesswoman still remains unresolved. Women considering a business visit to Saudi Arabia are advised to contact their Embassy for up-to-date advice.

5

getting down to business

5

getting down to business

This chapter provides elementary guidance on what kind of business can or cannot be done in the Kingdom, along with a brief look at some of the economic factors that might influence decisions on setting up an operation in the Kingdom. A few notes are provided which deal with the mechanics of getting your materials into the Kingdom along with pointers to specific organisations offering more information or assistance.

Trade Summary

In 1993, Saudi Arabia applied for accession to GATT (The General Agreement on Tariffs and Trade), which was established in 1947 by a group of 23 countries. GATT was the predecessor to the WTO (World Trade Organisation), whose purpose is to promote free trade by persuading countries to abolish import tariffs and other barriers.

5

In 1995, Saudi Arabia established an inter-ministerial working group to develop a WTO accession strategy setting the country on a long and arduous path of change and reform. The WTO has a much broader scope than GATT in that GATT regulated trade almost solely in goods, while WTO covers trade in services and other issues such as intellectual property rights.

At the heart of the WTO are the Agreements, negotiated and signed by the majority of the world's trading nations and ratified in their parliaments. The goal is to help producers of goods and services, exporters, and importers conduct their business. WTO decisions are absolute and every member must abide by the rulings.

Saudi Arabia became the 149th member of the WTO on 11 December 2005. During the process of accession Saudi Arabia extensively revised its trade regime to comply with WTO requirements, and is working to implement its commitments.

Saudi Arabia uses the Harmonised System (HS) codes of classifying products for trading purposes. As a member of the Gulf Cooperation Council, Saudi Arabia applies the GCC common external tariff of five per cent for most products, with a number of country-specific exceptions. Saudi Arabia's exceptions to the common external tariff include 400 HS coded products that may be imported duty-free, including aircraft and most livestock.

The Saudi government also applies a 12 per cent tariff on another 400 or so HS product codes, in some cases to protect local industries. Certain textile imports, including carpets but excluding apparel, are among the products to which this rate applies, as are certain industrial gases and chemicals, an assortment of building materials, specialised vehicles and toothbrushes. A number of Saudi industries enjoy 20 per cent tariff protection, including those producing oxygen, some wooden products and plastic pipes. In addition, long-life milk and about 20 other agricultural products and derivatives are subject to a 25 per cent tariff on a seasonal basis. Saudi Arabia imposes a 40 per cent tariff on dates and a 100 per cent tariff on cigarette and other tobacco imports including jirak (shisha), the sweetened tobacco used in water pipes.

A list of over 300 HS codes on the Civil Aviation commodity list are considered exempt from customs duties where they are imported exclusively for civil aviation purposes, even where the HS code is subject to a duty rate.

Saudi Arabia's complete tariff schedule is available online at www.customs.gov.sa.

General enquires are fielded by the Ministry of Finance's Saudi Arabian Department of Customs (SADC) offices in Riyadh
Tel +966 1 406 8953 ext 4456 Fax: +966 1 405 9282.

Import Licensing

In Saudi Arabia, the importation of certain articles is either entirely prohibited or requires special approval from competent authorities. Specifically, the importation of alcohol, chocolates or any other products containing alcohol, pork products, and frog's legs is prohibited. Imports of agriculture seeds, live animals, fresh and frozen meat, books, periodicals, movies, tapes, religious books and tapes, firearms, chemicals and harmful materials, pharmaceutical products, wireless equipment, radio-controlled model airplanes, natural asphalt, and archaeological artefacts require special approval.

The central governing body for customs administration in Saudi Arabia is the Directorate General for Customs Affairs, which operates under the Ministry of Finance. The Directorate General is based in Riyadh. There are three Customs Secretariats in Dammam, Gizan, and Jeddah. Each Secretariat is responsible for a number of Customs posts. In total, Saudi Arabia has 33 ports including airports, seaports and land (dry) ports. The same procedures for clearing customs apply in each port. Customs posts operate at the seaports of Diba, Yanbu, Jeddah and Gizan on the Red Sea; Ras Meshab, Ras Tanura, Jubail, Dhahran and Dammam on the Gulf Coast. Airport customs posts operate at King

Khalid International in Riyadh, King Abdulaziz Airport in Jeddah, King Fahd Airport in the Eastern Province as well as the airports at Taif, Abha, Madinah, Tabuk, Al Jouf, Hail and Qasim. Special dry ports also operate in Riyadh and Tabuk. The remainder are located on road crossings with neighbouring countries.

Only Saudi nationals or companies wholly owned by Saudi nationals have the right to import goods into Saudi Arabia for resale in the Saudi market or re-export. All company board members as well as the persons vested with power to sign must be Saudi nationals. The importer must be a Saudi national listed in the Commercial Register held by the Ministry of Commerce and Industry, and be in possession of a licence allowing the importer to engage in external trade related activities.

Reporting and Unloading Cargo

On arrival in Saudi Arabia, carriers are required to report their shipments by transmitting to the Customs authorities the original cargo manifest (with two Arabic copies). The manifest must show the quantities, marks, types, numbers and destination of the goods, the type of transportation facility, and the total number of packages in words and numbers; the manifest must agree with the contents of the cargo. Goods imported by land must have the manifest prepared at the point of origin or at the last customs point prior to crossing the Saudi border.

The original manifest (in duplicate) must be accompanied by a request for unloading in Arabic, and be authorised by the agent of the shipping company. These documents must be submitted within 36 hours of the vessel's arrival. Carriers may proceed to unload after permission is received. In the case of air shipments, Saudi Arabian Airlines is responsible for unloading the goods and storing them in a customs warehouse, while each port authority is responsible for unloading goods that are imported by sea. Receipt of the goods by customs takes place only when the cargo arrives at the customs warehouse or other designated storage area, and is externally inspected. Shipping companies are responsible for shortages until the goods are delivered into the customs warehouse. On delivery and inspection, the shipping company is provided with an official receipt. When goods arrive at any port in the Kingdom, and have been unloaded into a Customs warehouse, the importer or agent

5

is allowed 10 days in the case of goods imported by air and 13 days in the case of goods imported by sea to clear Saudi customs. If goods are not removed from customs at the end of this period, they are subject to demurrage charges.

On receipt of the customs file, Customs Control determines how the goods should be inspected. All shipments are inspected, fully, partially, or visually. The Customs Inspector may decide on specific procedures, such as sending the shipment for health inspection in the case of food products, by referring it for health, quality control, agricultural inspection or to the Saudi Arabian Standards Organisation (SASO) for conformity with Saudi standards. If none of these are required, the Customs Declaration Form is signed by the Inspector, and the broker pays the import charges.

While the importer will normally handle these procedures, if you are selling goods destined for Saudi Arabia it is as well to be advised of what those procedures are, so that you understand what you might be asked to provide.

Documentation Required

Originals of standard trade documents will include a Customs Import Declaration form, Commercial Invoice, Certificates of Origin and Insurance, Airway Bill or Bill of Lading, Steamship or Airline Certificate, Insurance Certificate, Packing List plus additional documentation depending on the type and nature of the goods. E.g. Halal certification is required for meat and food products. AQIS documentation and special certification applies for live animals and plants.

To export products to Saudi Arabia from the United States, the US Department of State's Authentication Division and the Saudi Embassy or Consulate must authenticate the documentation. The US-Saudi Arabian Business Council is not required to certify legal documents, but will do so if requested. Some products, most notably agricultural biotechnology products, need a certificate from the country of origin attesting to the product's fitness for human consumption and that it is sold widely in the country of origin. All consumer products must have a certificate of conformity issued under the guidelines of the Certificate of Conformity Program (COCP) before entering the country.

In the United Kingdom, the Arab British Chamber of Commerce can advise on appropriate certification as well as keeping you informed of any changes to the legislation regarding imports to the Kingdom.

The Saudi Arabian Standards Organization's (SASO) role, which previously included governance of certificates of conformity, is now limited to issuance of applicable Saudi standards for consumer products.

The documents required for all commercial shipments to the Kingdom of Saudi Arabia, irrespective of value or mode of transportation, are:

1: Commercial Invoice

All commercial invoices must be on the letterhead of the exporting company. The invoice should contain names and addresses of consignor and consignee, an accurate description of goods and components (trademarks, name of the vessel or airlines) and the date of sailing, port of loading and port of discharge, net and gross weight, quantity, unit price and extended price of each type of goods, total value of the shipment, contents of each package and container, currency, number of Letter of Credit (if applicable) and freight and insurance.

2: Certificate of Origin

The manufacturer (or the exporting firm) must issue this certificate. In addition to the name of the vessel (airline) and the date of sailing, name(s), nationality(ies), and full street address(es) of the manufacturer(s) of all items and components thereof, must be declared. Furthermore, the origin of each item or component must be specified. A signed statement to the effect that the document is true and correct must be given.

If the merchandise to be shipped to Saudi Arabia is not solely and exclusively originated in the exporting country then a notarised 'appended declaration to Certificate of Origin' (available at any Saudi Consulate), must be attached to the Certificate of Origin. In addition, the Certificate of Origin must include the name and address of the Saudi importer, a description of the goods, and the address of the shipping company.

3: Bill of Lading or an Airway Bill

One non-negotiable copy of the Bill of Lading is to be

5

presented to a Saudi Arabian Consulate. The Bill of Lading should agree with the Commercial Invoice and show description, value, and net and gross weight of shipped goods. Likewise, volume and measurement, marks, number of packages, name and address of Saudi importer and consignor, name and address of shipping company and/or shipping agent, name of vessel and date of sailing, port of loading and port of discharge, etc., should agree with those on invoice and containers

4: A steamship or an airlines Company Certificate

This certificate (which is an appended declaration to Bill of Lading or the Airway Bill) should be issued by the steamship (or airline) company in at least one original. It must be notarised and contain the following information about the vessel (or plane), named in the Bill of Lading or the airline company certificate:

- Name of vessel (plane) and previous name (if applicable).
- Nationality of vessel (plane).
- Owner of vessel (plane).
- Name(s) of ports (airports) that vessel (plane) will call on en route to Saudi Arabia

A: Port (airport) of loading ....
B: ....
C: ....
D: Port (airport) of discharge ....

Further, the steamship or airlines company certificate should declare that said vessel (plane) shall not anchor or call on any other ports (airports) than those mentioned in it, and that all information provided in the certificate is true and correct. The standard form of the Appended Declaration to the Bill of Lading or airway bill is available at any Saudi Arabian Consulate.

5: Insurance Certificate (if goods are insured by the exporter)

This certificate issued by an insurance company in at least one original, must contain the following information: actual amount of insurance, description and value of insured goods, name of vessel, port of loading and Saudi port of discharge, and name and address of beneficiary. Moreover, the appended declaration to insurance policy (form of which is available at any Saudi Arabian Consulate) should state that the insurance company has a duly qualified and appointed agent or representative in the Kingdom of Saudi Arabia, giving his name and full address. If an insurance company in Saudi Arabia insures the shipment, the exporter, on his letterhead, must state the name and address of said company.

6: Packing List

This includes names and addresses of consignor and consignee, description and value of the exported goods, net and total weight, number of packages and their contents, number of containers and contents, numbers of seals, and number of L/C (if applicable).

7: Other Documents

Depending on the nature of goods being shipped, or upon certain requests from the Saudi importer or in a Letter of Credit, or according to clauses in a contractual agreement, specific additional documents may also be required. The original of some documents must be accompanied by an Arabic translation.

Standards, Testing, Labelling Certification

Labelling and marking require special attention. This area is regulated by the Saudi Arabia Standards Organization (SASO). Stringent labelling standards apply to food, pharmaceuticals and personal care products. There are also strict requirements for expiry dates. Products may be rejected if less than half the time between production and expiration date remains.

In 2005 it was reported that Saudi Arabia abolished the International Conformity Certification Programme (ICCP), a pre-shipment certification programme initiated in 1995 to monitor and control the quality of certain products imported into the country. In place of ICCP, the certification programme is now under the control of the Certificate of Conformity Programme (COCP). The new programme requires all exporting companies to provide a certificate of conformity with every shipment to Saudi Arabia. The regulations pertaining to the new COCP had not been published at the time of writing. As a transitional measure, Saudi Arabia has implemented a temporary rule

5

that a certificate of conformity shall accompany every imported consumer product bound for Saudi Arabia. The COCP shall be signed by an approved laboratory in the country of origin specifying that the imported goods either abide by or meet applicable Saudi standards, if available, or adhere to international standards.

Saudi Arabia will utilize third-party laboratories to clear incoming shipments from customs after these laboratories are established and drafted regulations approved.

The new conformity certificates for goods exported to Saudi Arabia will apply to all products. The Ministry of Commerce and Industry is now the over-sight authority rather than SASO. More information may be obtained from the companies listed.

Intertek Testing Services (ITS)
Academy Place
1-9 Brook Street
Brentwood,
Essex CM14 5NQ
Tel: +44 (0)1277 223304 Fax: +44 (0)1277 220246
Website: www.intertek-fts.com

SGS United Kingdom Ltd
SGS House
217-221 London Road
Camberley
GU15 3EY
Surrey
Tel: +44 (0)1276 697 877 Fax: +44 (0)1276 697 696
Website: www.uk.sgs.com

The Saudi Arabian Standards Organization imposes shelf-life requirements on food products. In practice, the Saudi government requires imported food products to arrive in port with at least half their shelf life remaining, calculated from the date of production. Over the past few years, SASO has shortened the shelf life duration for baby foods, eggs, chilled meats, and some snack foods. Saudi Arabia requires an animal protein-free certificate for imports of poultry, beef, and lamb and their by-products. In addition, the Saudi Government bans the import of therapeutic medicines used in animal feed. In 2006 Saudi Arabia imposed a complete ban on live birds following the worldwide fear of a bird flu epidemic.

No medicines or pharmaceuticals are allowed into Saudi Arabia unless they are registered in advance with the Food and Pharmaceuticals Authority, under the Ministry of Health. The Ministry examines applications, which must be supported by the required certificates authenticated by the Saudi Consulate in the country of origin, and analyses the samples to ensure that they conform to the required specifications, before granting an import license. All shipments are checked by the Ministry of Health at the point of entry to the Kingdom.

5

Imports of medicines and pharmaceuticals also require a certificate from the responsible authority in the country of origin stating that these products are, in fact, used under the same brand name and formula in that country. This certificate must also be authenticated by the Saudi Consulate in the country of origin.

Special provisions apply to agricultural products such as nursery plants, plants, and all kinds of fruits, vegetables, and seeds. In addition to the general shipping documents, an exporter of such items to Saudi Arabia must submit the following to the Department of Agriculture before they are allowed into the country

- Certificate of Inspection issued by a company specialising in seed inspection
- Phytosanitary Certificate verifying that the seeds or grains are free from agricultural diseases
- Seed Analysis Certificate to prove the degree of purity of the seeds
- Certificate of Weight

All shipments of plants are inspected on arrival in the Kingdom.

Temporary Imports

Temporary clearance of goods is not permitted regardless of status as commercial goods or government imported goods. Customs formalities on the goods must be completed, inspection carried out, and duty paid at the point of entry to the Kingdom prior to the goods being allowed into the country.

'Duty Drawback' is a refund available in Saudi Arabia to the importer/exporter of record for raw material imports that are processed in the Kingdom and re-exported as

5

more finished goods. The Duty Drawback Scheme is usually used when duty exemptions are not available on the goods in question.

To trigger Duty Drawback status, importers or their agents must inform Customs at the point of entry that the imported goods are raw materials that will be further processed and re-exported. The importer will pay the duty assessed on importation, but the amount is kept in bond and refunded on re-export of the goods. Prior to re-export, the exporter must submit all export documentation together with a copy of the Customs Import Declaration, a receipt for payment of duty on the raw materials, the Certificate of Origin, and a copy of the invoice to the buyer certified by the Chamber of Commerce. Customs use a standard formula to determine how much of the imported raw material is used in the final exported product. The same formula is applied to every product.

Exports

Exporting goods from the Kingdom is relatively simple. An Export Certificate and a Customs Declaration must be completed for all goods. Following submission of these documents to the Director of Customs, who authorizes the export, they are sent to the Valuation Division, which stamps them, registers them, provides a serial number and endorses the shipment for inspection. The goods are not allowed to enter the Customs area until the out-of-Kingdom means of transportation is already in the port, and a shipment inspection and valuation is completed by a representative of the Customs Department.

Government Procurement

Saudi Arabia agreed to become an observer to the WTO Government Procurement Agreement and to initiate negotiations on membership as part of its accession to the WTO. Several Royal Decrees strongly favouring GCC nationals apply to Saudi Arabia's government procurement contracts. However, most defence contracts are negotiated outside these regulations on a case-by-case basis. Under a 1983 Royal Decree, contractors must subcontract 30 per cent of the value of any government contract, including support services, to firms majority-owned by Saudi nationals. An exemption is granted in instances where no Saudi-owned company can provide the goods and services necessary to fulfil the procurement requirement.

Foreign suppliers that participate in government projects are required to establish a training programme for Saudi nationals. Some government contracts will also require a minimum level of subcontracting with Saudi companies.

5

In addition, the Saudi Government may favour joint venture companies with a Saudi partner over foreign firms and will also support companies that use Saudi goods and services. For large military projects, there is frequently an offset requirement; this is determined on a project-by-project basis.

Foreign companies providing services to the Saudi Arabian government can do so without a Saudi service agent and can market their services to various other public entities directly through a temporary registration office. Foreign contractors working only for the government, if not already registered to do business in Saudi Arabia, are required to obtain temporary registration from the Ministry of Commerce and Industry within 30 days of contract signing. Foreign companies also are allowed to establish a branch office through new Foreign Investment Regulations. These branch offices are usually approved only for foreign defence contractors and high-technology companies. For others, a liaison office may be established to supervise work in Saudi Arabia and to facilitate coordination between the Saudi government and company headquarters

In June 2003, the Saudi Council of Ministers passed a resolution calling for increased transparency in government-budgeted projects and government contracts. The contract information to be made public includes: title, parties, date, financial value, brief description, duration, place of execution, and point of contact information. The Council of Saudi Chambers of Commerce and Industry and the Ministry of Finance have begun publishing the details of government contracts on its website.

5

Intellectual Property Rights (IPR) Protection

In 2006 Saudi Arabia enacted laws covering a range of IPR issues, including patents, trademarks, copyright, trade names, commercial data, border protection of IPR, and protection of confidential commercial information. The laws also increased penalties for violators, including fines and prison sentences. Saudi Arabia has made progress on copyright enforcement over the past few years, with a steadily increasing number of raids/seizures and fines imposed. However, some items like computer software are still easily obtained on the streets of most cities.

Although Saudi Arabia has passed new patent legislation and in recent years has taken measures to hire and train more examiners, translators, and clerks, the processing of patent applications has historically suffered from extreme delays. Patent registration is open to individuals and corporate bodies, both Saudi and foreign. However, a patent applicant is required to have a local agent. Applications are submitted to the King Abdulaziz City for Science and Technology (KACST). Every patent is valid for 15 years and renewable for an additional period of five years. The patent and trademark regulations have been reviewed and the new laws will subject Saudi Arabia to the standards and obligations of the Agreement on Trade-Related Aspects of Intellectual Property.

Shipping

Saudi Arabia gives preferences to national carriers for up to 40 per cent of government related cargoes. Under these rules, the National Shipping Company of Saudi Arabia and United Arab Shipping Company have preference.

Agent and Distributor Rules

Saudi law requires that domestic distributors register with the Ministry of Commerce and Industry. Currently, only Saudi citizens can obtain registration as distributors. A recent GCC decision may broaden this to make all GCC citizens eligible. Nationals from the GCC countries are also allowed to engage in trading and retail activities, including real estate. By the same token, foreign nationals are allowed to own real estate on a limited basis. Saudi Arabia's WTO commitments, which came into effect on

11 December 2005, open distribution to non-nationals on a gradual basis, up to 75 per cent of total equity within three years. In July 2001, the Saudi Council of Ministers cancelled the requirement for foreign companies with government contracts to have a Saudi service agent.

Business Entities

According to the Executives Rules of the Foreign Investment Act, foreign investors may conduct business in Saudi Arabia in one of the following forms:

A. Limited Liability Company (LLC)

This is the most common form for entering into joint ventures. An LLC must have between 2 and 50 shareholders and is managed and represented by one or more managers. There is no Board of Directors, although shareholders often provide for a Board and other management arrangements in the Memorandum of Association. The LLC must also have an auditor and, where it has more than twenty (20) partners; it must establish a Board of Controllers.

B. Partnerships

The limited partnership is a separate business entity comprised of several individuals or companies. The general partners are liable for partnership debts to the full extent of their personal assets while the limited partners are liable only to the extent of their capital contributions. Foreign companies may enter into a limited partnership.

C. Branch Offices

Foreign companies may register a wholly foreign-owned Saudi branch office, provided that they obtain the requisite license. The branch office may engage in any government contract or private sector work within the scope of its license. Branch offices are subject to the requirements of the Government Tenders Regulations, where applicable. Branch office registration follows the same general procedure as for the registration of an LLC.

D. Commercial Agencies

The rules and regulations reserve a monopoly for Saudi nationals and wholly owned Saudi entities on trading activities. Trading activities include the import and local purchase of goods for resale. Therefore, foreign

5

companies engaging in such activities must use Saudi commercial agents and distributors, who must register their Agency Agreements with the MOC Agency Register. The agent must hold a valid Saudi commercial registration permitting him to act as an agent or distributor and the directors and authorized representatives of the agent must be Saudi nationals.

E. Franchising

Franchising is becoming popular and growing day by day. It helps establish consumer-oriented businesses in Saudi Arabia.

Investment

In April 2000, Saudi Arabia's Council of Ministers approved a new foreign direct investment code with the goal of facilitating establishment of foreign companies, both joint ventures and 100 per cent foreign-owned, in Saudi Arabia. Key provisions allow foreign investors to transfer money freely into and out of the country, allow joint-venture companies to sponsor their foreign investors as well as their foreign employees (all foreigners in Saudi Arabia need a legal sponsor in order to reside in the country), and permit foreign investors to own real estate for company activities.

The Saudi Arabian General Investment Authority (SAGIA) was established to manage investments under the new code, with guidance from the Supreme Economic Council. In addition to its existing Service Centres, in March 2003, SAGIA opened a Women's Investment Centre. In principle, SAGIA must decide to grant or refuse a license within 30 days of receiving an application and supporting documentation from the investor. Wholly domestic projects funded with Saudi money do not need licenses through SAGIA's investment services centre, which was specifically designed for foreign investors. However, many of the licenses are issued for projects jointly owned with Saudi investors. Some foreign investors have complained that the licensing process was not as streamlined as SAGIA intended. Impediments, often caused by other Ministries' bureaucracy, frequently delayed the application process. SAGIA continues to take steps to address these difficulties, including making separate agreements in 2005 with other Ministries and government agencies to facilitate foreign investment.

While SAGIA is intended to operate as a one-stop shop, where foreign investors can obtain all of the necessary permits or authorizations, some companies still experience delays in subsequent steps, for example in obtaining a commercial registry or purchasing property.

Following SAGIA's recommendations, the Supreme Economic Council published in 2001 a negative list of sectors in which foreign investment is prohibited. The list can be inspected for changes at www.sagia.gov.sa.

5

The law permits foreigners to invest in all sectors of the economy, except for specific activities contained in the negative list. In respect to the capital requirements needed, these are as follows:

SR100,000 for individual establishments
SR500,000 for companies
SR1,000,000 for industrial projects
SR25,000,000 for agricultural projects

Negative List as at August 2006. The activities that are not open to foreign investors are:

Manufacturing Sector

1   Oil exploration, drilling and production. Except the services related to mining sector listed at (5115+883) in International Industrial classification codes.

2   Manufacturing of military equipment, devices and uniforms.

3   Manufacturing of civilian explosives.

Service Sector

1   Catering to military sectors.

2   Security and detective services.

3   Real estate investment in Makkah and Madinah.

4   Tourist orientation and guidance services related to Hajj and Umrah.

5   Recruitment and employment services including local recruitment offices.

6   Real estate brokerage.

7   Printing and publishing. Except the following activities:

- Pre-printing services internationally classified at 88442

- Printing Presses internationally classified at 88442

- Drawing and calligraphy internationally classified at 87501

- Photography internationally classified at 875

- Radio and Television Broadcasting Studios internationally classified at 96114

- Foreign Media Offices and Correspondents internationally classified at 962

- Promotion and Advertising internationally classified at 871

- Public Relations internationally classified at 86506

- Publication internationally classified at 88442

- Press Services internationally classified at 88442

- Production, selling and renting of computer software internationally classified at 88

- Media consultancies and studies internationally classified at 853

- Typing and Xeroxing internationally classified at (87505 + 87904).

8   Distribution services, wholesale and retail trade including medical retail services and private pharmacies internationally classified at (631+632+6111+6113+6121). Also commercial agencies, except franchise rights listed at (8929) by international industrial classifications.

9   Audiovisual and media services.

10 Telecommunications services, except the following activities:

- Telex services internationally classified at 7523

- Telegraph services internationally classified at 7522

- Electronic Data Interchange (EDI) internationally classified at 7523

- Enhanced/value-added facsimile services, including storage, forwarding, and retrieving internationally classified at 7523

- VSAT services internationally classified at 75291

- Fax services internationally classified at 7521 + 7529

- GMPCS services internationally classified at 75299

- Internet Service Provider (ISP) services internationally classified at 75299

- Electronic Mail internationally classified at 7523

- Provision of online information and database retrieval internationally classified at 7523

- Information provision and online retrieval and/or processing, including transaction processing internationally classified at 843

11   Land and air transportation.

12   Satellite transmission services.

13   Services rendered by midwives, nurses, physiotherapists and paramedics listed at 93191 by international classification codes.

14   Fisheries.

15   Blood banks, poison centres and quarantines.

In October 2003, the Saudi Government passed the Capital Markets Law, which took effect in February 2004. The law allows for the creation of financial intermediaries (stock brokerages and investment banks) and creates an independent stock market and an independent stock market regulatory body. The law sets SR5O million ($13.3 million) capitalization requirements for brokerages and provides penalties for insider trading and wrongful dissemination of information.

The law also allows for the development of long-term investment instruments and limits to 49 per cent the maximum equity share that may be held by foreign investment banking and brokerage firms that establish joint ventures with Saudi entities. Saudi Arabia agreed to raise the percentage of the foreign partner to 60 per cent after WTO accession. The new law does not repeal the prohibition on direct foreign participation in the Saudi stock market. Foreigners can continue to purchase shares in bank operated investment funds, however. Foreign participation in these funds is limited to 10 per cent of the total value of the fund.

5

6

Jeddah Islamic Seaport

major industries

major industries

This chapter gives an overview on the countries major business sectors and where they stand today.

Industry Overviews

The Saudi economy is witnessing a period of relatively high growth and economic progress. This is based upon a very strong oil sector, which is bringing in record oil revenue and allowing the Kingdom to increase public spending on infrastructure and welfare to match the increasing needs of the Saudi population. In turn the non-oil private sector is feeding off the upturn in public spending.

Saudi Arabia continues to pursue two principal economic goals. The first is economic diversification aimed at decreasing the country's dependence on oil through the development of industry and agriculture. The second is the transfer of economic growth responsibility to the private sector.

6

To achieve the first objective, the Saudi government continues to encourage joint ventures with foreign participation and management, especially those that can develop into enterprises managed and operated by Saudis.

Saudi Arabia offers an increasingly varied and sophisticated marketplace. Except for the obvious restrictions in certain product areas (e.g. alcohol and pork-related products) almost anything that can be bought or sold elsewhere in the world can be bought or sold in the Kingdom.

The sustained high level of oil prices has fuelled the Kingdoms appetite for 'mega' projects. The largest of these private sector developments is to be the King Abdullah Economic City, which will be developed by Dubai-based Emaar Properties in collaboration with Aseer and Binladen Group of Saudi Arabia in a joint venture called Emaar the Economic City. Two similar projects are the Prince Abdulaziz bin Musaed Economic City in Hail and the Knowledge City in Madinah.

According to the Samba Financial Group's mid-year report in 2006 about the Saudi economy, the total cost of projects currently under way or in advanced planning for execution over the next several years is about SR1.06 trillion ($283 billion). The oil and gas industry alone accounts for SR259b ($69b), or one fourth, of the total.

Accurate and detailed market data is sometimes difficult to source, with the result that frequently the best research is carried out by talking informally to as many relevant people as possible. The information gathered in this way cannot always be backed by statistics, but if the sources are numerous, diverse and informed, they should help to build a more accurate picture.

Agriculture

A strategic decision was taken in the early 1980s to develop an agricultural sector and, as a result, Saudi Arabia is self sufficient in many fresh foods. Heavy subsidies given in previous years have been significantly reduced and as a result many of the production figures have changed significantly.

The SR3,500/ton subsidy level for wheat in the 1980s has been reduced to SR1000 today. From a position of being the world's 7th largest exporter of wheat in 1989, Saudi Arabia's production fell in 2005 to a position where imports were being considered. Also in 2005, Saudi Arabia was one of the world's largest importers of barley at between 4 and 6 million metric tons. Barley is mostly consumed as animal feed, but local production is limited, it being severely affected by seasonal rainfall variations. The Kingdom is now a large producer of corn, producing almost a million tons in 2005. Bizarrely this makes the Kingdom a good market for corn drying equipment. Importers receive a subsidy for corn imports of SR160/ton due to its use as feed.

Poultry production in 2006 is estimated at around 490,000 metric tons but the country still imports another 440,000 metric tons to satisfy demand. Poultry imports from the Far East were banned in 2005 due to the fears over bird flu, and by far the largest supply source is now Brazil, with France taking a significant position. Poultry consumption is predicted to continue rise. One of the larger farms operating about 50 kms north of Jeddah (Rabwa Group of Companies) now has a capacity of 28 million chickens per annum and occupies an area of about 16 sq kms. The largest company in the Middle East, Al Watania Poultry in Qassim employs over 6,500 people over 116 farms and has a production of half a million birds and a million eggs per day! The Kingdom is almost at the top of the list in consumption terms, getting through an average of 48kg per capita per annum.

6

The Ministry of Agriculture banned imports of biotech seeds in 2004 and no biotech crops are grown in the country, however imports of biotech grain and plant/vegetable based foodstuffs are permitted provided they are labelled as such.

Dairy figures for Saudi Arabia continue to be staggering compared to the rest of the world. Not only is Almarai planning to increase the size of its herd to approximately 48,000 milking cows, the Safi dairy, handling 26,000 milkers, is the largest single integrated unit in the world today. Milk demand is growing at about 4 per cent per annum and these two producers handle about 60 per cent of the market with another 25 per cent split between the Nadec and Nada Dairy companies. In 2006 fresh milk from Saudi Arabia was available in almost all neighbouring countries as well as some more distant, with reports of it being marketed in Libya. Despite these figures, the Kingdom still imports hundreds of thousands of tons of dairy products every year.

6

The Saudi market for rice is large and growing. The country relies on imports to cover all its needs for this staple food product. India is the dominant force in this market with about 65 per cent of the market share, followed by the United States at about a 12 per cent. Indian suppliers aggressively compete with US suppliers in both price and promotional activities. Other competitors include Pakistan (11 per cent), Thailand (8 per cent) and Australia (3 per cent). According to the Arab News in 2005, the Kingdom has over 200 rice importers, although only a few of them, including Al Muhaidib, Al Shaalan and Babakar, control three quarters of market share.

Dates are significant both in the local market and on the world stage. Considered the world's largest producer at over 800,000 tons per annum, it produces about 20 per cent of world production.

The demand for processed fruits and vegetables in Saudi Arabia is substantial. The growth of supermarket food sales is helping to broaden the market, and good market growth is expected to continue. Local production of canned fruits and vegetables has been on the increase, however, insufficient local fruit and vegetable output and the high costs related to importing them for use in local

6

processing suggest that a significant demand for processed fruits and vegetables will continue to be met by imports.

The last official census indicated that more than 60 per cent of the Saudi population are in their teens, a group which is a significant consumer of snack foods. Local production of snack foods has dramatically increased in recent years. Leading companies have realised the potential of the snack market and have launched massive production units. There is a general decline in imports of corn-and wheat-based snacks. Sweets and chocolates are also being manufactured on a large scale. However, the scope for quality branded chocolates and snacks still exists, as does raw material and production machinery for the sector

Agricultural Production Statistics for 1995	
PRODUCE	TONS
Cereals	2,170,794
Dates	734,844
Fruit	1,188,460
Vegetables	1,927,013
Wheat	1,787,542
Source: www.saudinf.com	

Auto Parts and Service Equipment

Saudi Arabia has one of the world's highest per capita spending on vehicles. It is the largest and most sophisticated car market in the Middle East. Gone are the days when almost-new cars would be abandoned on the highway because of the lack of spares. Analysts anticipate that during the next decade the age of vehicles on the road will increase from five to ten years, and with this increase in automobile life, the market for spare parts is expected to expand significantly. The size of the market is estimated between $300 and $500 million by some industry analysts, while others put the sales of auto spares, accessories and garage equipment at $2.3 billion. There are over 6 million vehicles on the Saudi roads.

US and Japanese motors dominate the market with German and Korean imports more in evidence in recent years. European imports are generally restricted to the luxury market with certain models considered status symbols. Despite the recent reduction in fuel costs, engine capacities and fuel consumption figures may become more relevant and the future composition of vehicle imports will, to a large extent, dictate the mix of the auto parts industry. As additional makes and models are introduced, the Saudi spare parts market will expand accordingly. The market is already competitive, and becoming increasingly so with a growing demand for original as opposed to counterfeit spares.

6

Reported in the Arab News on 1 May 2006

"In order to improve the living standard of citizens and for the public good, we have ordered that the price of one litre of petrol for the consumer be changed to 60 hallalas instead of 90 hallalas until Dec. 31, 2006," a Royal Decree stated.

The Decree said the price of 91-octane petrol for consumers would be brought down to 60 hallalas from 82 hallalas per litre while price of 95-octane petrol would be slashed from SR1.02 to 75 hallalas, effective from 1 January 2007.

King Abdullah also cut diesel prices from 37 to 25 hallalas per litre.

60 hallalahs was about 8 and half pence! At the same time the UK price for fuel was hovering around 95 pence per litre.

Banking

The Saudi banking sector and, by extension, the Saudi consumer, have never had it so good. With an economy boosted by sky-high oil prices and revenues, it is not surprising that national income continues to grow.

According to SAMA, at the end of September 2005, Saudi commercial banks had a total of 1,240 branches throughout the Kingdom. There were 4,413 ATMs in the Kingdom by the end of September 2005, which processed 45,386,900 transactions worth SR22.65 billion. In the

6

same period, Saudi banks had issued a total of 7,557,353 bankcards of various descriptions and uses.

With all these market dynamics, competition in the retail and consumer finance services market is toughening up, even though the cake is getting bigger all the time, given the age and consumer demographics of the Kingdom. Some 70 per cent of Saudis are under 25 years of age. As such, for banks and consumer companies Saudi Arabia represents effectively a captive market. There are also those who stress that Saudi Arabia is still under-banked, both in terms of products and services in terms of consumer choice and in terms of competition and market access, especially to foreign players.

Under the WTO accession rules, commercial presence of foreign banks in the Kingdom will be permitted in the form of a locally incorporated joint stock company or as a branch of an international bank. The foreign equity cap for joint ventures in banking is 60 per cent. While financial services can only be provided by commercial banks, asset management and advisory services may also be provided by non-commercial banking financial institutions.

The emergence of foreign competition will have paradoxically a positive and negative effect on the Saudi domestic banking market. Local banks will be forced to refine and improve their services and products — in pricing, flexibility, delivery, and after-sales services — to meet the standards especially of the banking majors such as HSBC, Deutsche Bank and Citigroup. On the other hand, the smaller Saudi banks may feel the pinch and be forced even further into niche markets.

Islamic banking is the fastest growing market segment in the Kingdom and the Gulf region and competition is set to be fierce in this sector. Already NCB, the largest bank in Saudi Arabia and the Middle East and North Africa (MENA) region in terms of balance sheet, has already announced that it is in the process of converting its entire retail banking function into Islamic retail banking.

Clothing

Saudi Arabia offers a growing market for Western suppliers, particularly for European branded products. The US share of the Saudi apparel market is low compared to European and southeast Asian products although it may increase with changing shopping opportunities. A number of French and Italian boutiques have emerged in Saudi Arabia, specialising in particular brands or styles. Contributing factors to the shopping spree include an above-average population growth figure of about just under 3 per cent; three to four million pilgrims who visit Islam's holy sites in Makkah and Madinah every year and exposure to a selection of over 250 satellite television channels from around the world.

Construction

6

The changing skylines of Jeddah's corniche and in Riyadh, with its Al-Faisaliah and Kingdom Towers, are witness to the acceleration in construction activity throughout the Kingdom in recent years. More than $1 billion of hotel and office building projects in Riyadh alone are being developed. The building boom is also being spurred by planned government investments to expand the country's electricity network and water supplies. Just the construction element attached to power supply development is estimated at nearly $700 million. In total, current infrastructure and public sector building programmes are valued at some $35 billion. Plans include building 600 new factories, schools, doubling desalination capacity, increasing electrical generation and distribution. Some two million new homes are to be built in the next four years with many more planned.

There is particularly high demand for housing in the capital, Riyadh. One estimate is that overall the Kingdom will need to go much further than planned with its housing programmes, both government and privately sponsored. Some estimates calculate a need to double the number of houses and apartments to 9 million in the next 15 years to cope with projected demand.

Tourism is another emerging sector providing substantial construction work. A $1 billion seafront venture over 3.4 million square metres of reclaimed land between Al-Khobar and Dammam is planned to provide houses, apartments, hotels, a marina, shopping, and a man-made lagoon.

Electricity Generation

Saudi Arabia has one of the highest per capita electricity consumption rates in the world (average 5,000 Kw

6

Hr/month). The number of subscribers increased from 351,531 in 1975 to over 4.5 million at present. Since 1990, total electricity capacity has been increasing at a slower rate than demand. The power network has not developed evenly throughout the Kingdom, and some rural areas not yet connected to the power network.

Saudi Arabia needs to expand its power capacity and network to support the Kingdom's ambitious industrialisation plan. The Ministry of Water and Electricity's 25 year (1995-2020) electrification plan calls for US $117 billion in capital investment to increase total capacity from about 17,000 Mw per year at the beginning of the plan to 67,000 Mw by the year 2020.

Many power projects have been launched to achieve this expansion, both by upgrading existing power plants and building new power facilities. In 2000, Saudi Arabia's ten regional power companies were consolidated into a single joint-stock company, the Saudi Electricity Company (SEC), in order to streamline the sector's operations.

Besides power generation, Saudi Arabia requires additional investment in power transmission. Currently only two of the country's four power regions are connected. Creating a unified grid could require over 20,000 miles of additional power lines. Saudi Arabia and the other five GCC states plan to link the electrical power networks.

Environmental Technology

The Government allocated $267 million for environmental protection and pollution control in the 2007 budget. In addition, a substantial amount of the $2 billion budget of the Ministry of Municipality & Housing has been set aside for the handling, processing, managing and disposal of solid waste.

All new major industrial projects in the Kingdom now require Environmental Impact Assessments (EIA) at the planning and feasibility study stage, without which a license will not be issued. Local companies also lack specialised knowledge in areas of pollution control such as:
- Environmental Monitoring
- Environmental Analytical services
- Environmental Engineering & Consultancy
- Hazardous Waste Management
- Site remediation and rehabilitation

According to a recent independent study, the Arabian Gulf marine pollution constitutes about 30 per cent of the world's oil pollution. Oil tanker movement is the main cause.

In many areas, Saudi Arabia may still be characterised as a developing nation, and the market for pollution control equipment and services is promising. Urban development and industrial growth have compounded Saudi Arabia's environmental problems. Population growth, a significant construction market, sustainable growth of Saudi Arabia's oil, gas and petrochemical industry, the rising level of ground water, an inadequate sewerage system, increasing air pollution and solid waste, have all contributed toward making the Saudi environmental technology market a promising one.

There is severe lack of expertise in the field of wastewater treatment, which has led to a marked increase in water pollution in the Kingdom. Wastewater collection and treatment systems exist in only 22 out of 106 Municipal areas, and some major towns and cities have no piped collection systems as yet. It is estimated that of all the wastewater collected, only one third is to the tertiary standard required by regulation for reuse. Many of the existing plants are obsolete and need rehabilitation. A major construction programme of wastewater treatment plants is needed to increase capacity. A study by the Ministry of Water and Electricity estimates that Saudi Arabia will need to invest about US$20 billion for building new sewer networks and about US$17 billion on new waste treatment plants in the next 20 years.

Food

Saudi Arabia alone accounts for more than 63per cent of the GCC's total annual food imports estimated at US$10 billion, out of the Middle East's total of US$30 billion annual imports. The leading importers of foods and drinks are based in Jeddah and Riyadh, where more than 70 per cent of the imported food products are received through Jeddah Islamic Port. Market demand for all types of dairy products in Saudi Arabia is estimated at over SR11 billion.

Because of the harsh climate and insufficient arable land, limited water supplies and a growing population, it is

6

likely that the Kingdom will remain dependent on foreign suppliers for a wide range of fresh and processed food products. As consumer demands and tastes develop, there will be an increasing demand for niche and novelty products, (e.g. energy drinks) and products with strong and well-developed brands. All types of flavouring, special additives, juice concentrate and other ingredients for the food processing industry have good potential.

Information Technology

The IT sector is one targeted for growth by the Saudi government. Total IT expenditure is estimated around $3 billion per annum, which represents about 50 per cent of GCC expenditure. The split is now reckoned to be roughly 80:20 between hardware and software. The arrival in Saudi Arabia of the Internet service has continued to fuel demand for computers in Saudi homes and small businesses. Efficient network solutions are becoming a more important issue within the local business community. Smaller businesses are investigating the advantages of acquiring and installing efficient client/server configurations to help them increase work productivity and cut communication costs.

Local vendors are vying for better positions in various niches by offering more technologically advanced computers with added features at ever-cheaper prices. Several third-country manufacturers, especially from Southeast Asia, are active in the market. With over 300 local dealers selling various computer brands throughout Saudi Arabia, a number of them now offer locally assembled equipment.

The biggest customers are reputed to be banks and the hotels although Saudi Aramco, the Kingdom's oil company, is still considered to be the largest buyer of computers in the whole Gulf region. The national airline is another major and regular purchaser of equipment. Several other industry sectors are eager to modernise their computer and communication systems.

Software piracy remains a problem and, although the Saudi Government is committed to enforcing regulations to curbing illegal reproduction of computer software, almost any programme is available on the streets for a fraction of the price of the original.

6

Insurance

Saudi Arabia is the largest market in the GCC area and the second largest in the Arab world. The insurance market was estimated to be about SR4 billion in 2006 with car insurance holding the largest share at 32 per cent, followed by medical insurance at 22 per cent, property insurance at 17 per cent and others at 29 per cent. Estimates are that the market would exceed SR15 billion by 2009 as a result of the growing demand for medical and car insurance policies. Car insurance is expected to grow to SR5 billion and medical insurance to SR6.3 billion within the next four years.

In 1999, the Saudi government passed a number of regulations restricting resident expatriate access to public hospitals with the intention of passing on the cost to private insurance companies in the form of new co-operative medical insurance. In July 2003, the Saudi Council of Ministers passed legislation opening the insurance sector to foreign investment. From 1 June 2005 it became mandatory for all Saudi companies with a non-Saudi workforce of 500 or more expatriates to provide them with medical insurance. The second phase will involve companies with 100 to 500 staff and third stage with companies up to 100 staff.

The Saudi Arabian Monetary Agency (SAMA) had been entrusted with the responsibility of selecting the insurance companies and issuing them with the licences to cover medical insurance for the estimated six million expatriates in the Kingdom. They have since licensed a number of Saudi and foreign companies to provide this service although legal procedures were still pending in mid 2006. With the government decision to limit foreign ownerships in the operating companies to 60 per cent and require them to offer the remaining 40 per cent to the public, the insurance sector is set to be another spur in the country's economic development.

Medical Equipment

The Ministry of Health is the largest buyer of medical equipment, representing around 60 per cent of the market. It is also the major buyer on all GCC healthcare equipment and supplies tenders issued. In its 2006 budget, health and social development sector received SR31 billion for health services and social development,

6

nearly 14 per cent higher than the budgetary outlays of SR27.1 billion in 2005. This budget makes SR 4.3 billion allocations for the establishment of 24 new hospitals and for expansion, development & furnishing of existing health facilities in addition to establishing and furnishing of 440 primary healthcare centres in all the 13 regions of the Kingdom.

Healthcare in Saudi Arabia is increasingly being shared with public and private agencies. According to available figures, in 2003 the total number of hospitals in the Saudi health sector stood at 335. MOH had 194 with 28,510 beds, the private sector had 101 with 9,834 beds and other Government agencies accounted for another 40 with 9,576 beds. The MOH also operates around 1,792 primary healthcare centres and 19 dental centres, one in each health region, 5 chest hospitals, 3 tuberculosis centres and 8 rehabilitation centres. The private sector operates a further 800 clinics, 70 per cent of which are located in Jeddah and Riyadh.

Minerals and Mining

The mining sector has remained the untapped jewel in Saudi economic development, and it is here that Saudi investment efforts could be concentrated for a more viable and long-term sustainable economic growth. The geology of the Kingdom can be divided into two main zones. The Shield area in the west, adjacent to the Red Sea, covers one-third of the Kingdom and is the focus of gold and base metals exploration and mining. The surrounding sedimentary rocks dip gently toward the Arabian Gulf and contain industrial minerals, as well as being the reservoirs of the Kingdom's prolific oil and gas fields.

Saudi Arabia has the largest mineral deposits in the Middle East and the Ministry of Mineral Resources is reported to have located over 1,200 sites of precious metals and 1,200 sites of non-precious metals. Over 30 minerals have already been identified in the Kingdom, with at least 15 industrial minerals that could be successfully exploited by investors. More than 64 mining projects offering investment opportunities for private investors have also been identified. Deposits include gold, silver, copper, lead, zinc, iron, bauxite, phosphates, beryl, magnesium, salt and sulphur. Minerals are found both onshore and in the Red Sea where the Saudi-Sudan Red

Sea Exploration Commission has found substantial quantities of silver, zinc and copper.

Saudi Arabia's first commercial gold mine began operating in 1988. With four mines now operating, current gold production is about 350,000 ounces a year and is expected to double when two new mines open in the next few years.

Minerals are extracted not just for export, but can, and do, create clusters of industries turning minerals into products and generating employment. Plans for mining and related processing plants are ambitious, and it is believed that this sector will become a major source of revenue for the Kingdom during the next decade.

6

About $2.6 billion is currently being spent on two mining development projects and within the next five years the Kingdom is expected to become one of the world's leading producers of phosphate fertilizers and aluminium, which will be much in demand as the markets of China and India develop. The Kingdom has phosphate deposits to last 100 years and forecasts that the new bauxite project will enable production of 620,000 tons of aluminium annually. A crucial element in both projects is a $2 billion new 1,500 km-long railway to carry raw materials from phosphate mines at Al Jalamid, near the Iraq border, and bauxite from Al Zabira in the northeast. The Al Jalamid deposit alone is estimated to contain 313 million tonnes of phosphates able to provide sustained production for at least 27 years. Other major phosphate deposits have been identified in the area. The Al Zabira deposit is said to contain more than 240 million tonnes of bauxite.

Some $25 billion of investment is projected for the new city at Ras Al Zour which is planned to accommodate a range of downstream small and medium scale industries utilising both processed minerals production and petrochemical inputs from Jubail. Ras Al Zour could also become a centre for processing other locally available minerals such as silica, magnetite, dolomite and many others.

The Saudi Arabian Mining Company (Maaden) is responsible for regulating the mining sector, as well as consolidating mining projects that are wholly or partially owned by the Government. The new mining investment law approved in 2004 has simplified and streamlined the procedure for obtaining exploration and mining licenses and offers investors benefits including tax-free import of equipment and the right to obtain multiple licenses. Profits and capital may now be repatriated without restriction. The Chief Executive of Maaden has declared publicly that the next stage of development will be the privatisation of mining activities. It is further understood that the Saudi Government plans to offer 50 per cent of the company to the public in 2006/7.

Oil, Gas and Petrochemicals

Oil production was started in 1938 by the Arabian American Oil Company, now Saudi Aramco, the world's largest fully integrated oil company. It is generally acknowledged that Saudi Arabia has 25 per cent of the world's proven oil reserves. Saudi Aramco has now embarked on a massive expansion of its capabilities to meet the global increase in oil demand. At a meeting in April 2005 between the then Crown Prince Abdullah and President Bush, the Saudis announced they would be spending US$50 billion over the next five year period to boost Saudi oil production 10 million bpd to 12.5 million bpd. To put this increase in regional perspective, the total production capacity of the UAE is 2.5 million bpd. This increase in production is coupled with an increase in exploration. Saudi Arabia has only fully explored 25 per cent of its potential oil producing area. The aim of the latest round of exploration is to increase the proven oil reserves by 2010 by a further 100 billion barrels, from 260 billion to 360 billion barrels.

Saudi Arabia has the fourth largest proven gas reserves in the world. The much-heralded Gas Initiative of 2001 was scrapped after two years of haggling, but by 2006 Saudi Arabia had embarked on a massive programme to tap its gas reserves and is optimistic about major gas discoveries by the global energy giants in its vast Empty Quarter desert. The South Rub Al Khali Company (SRAK), a new $2.5 billion joint venture between Saudi Aramco, Royal Dutch Shell and France's Total, is exploring for gas in the area. The concession covers an area of nearly 210,000 sq kms of desert. Shell controls 40 per cent in SRAK, the balance being shared equally by Total and Aramco. The venture has been given five years for its exploration programme, but the period is extendable under a deal signed last year.

Another major concession was awarded in 2006 to a consortium of Russian, Chinese, Italian and Spanish companies covering 120,000 sq kms in the Rub Al Khali desert. Saudi Arabia already has a reserve of some six trillion cubic meters of natural gas which is expected to increase substantially with new discoveries in Rub Al Khali.

SABIC is the largest petrochemical company in the Middle East, the seventh largest globally, and Saudi Arabia's most successful listed company – recently ranked 22nd in the FT Global 500. They have announced a capital programme of US$8 billion to increase annual production from 48 million tonnes per annum to 60 million. In addition, there are many other companies with investments in petrochemical facilities in Jubail and Yanbu that aim to come on stream in the next three years.

With the vast investment in this sector most opportunities would be with Aramco and/or SABIC, both of which require an investment in time spent on the ground in Saudi Arabia. In addition to their capital spend, Saudi Aramco spends US$3.5 billion a year on goods and services.

Industry analysts estimate a five per cent annual growth rate for oil and gas equipment and materials. The demand for oil and gas products and services fluctuates yearly with the world price of oil; however, the operation and maintenance of facilities requires parts, and materials and services regardless of these fluctuations.

Pharmaceuticals

Saudi Arabia is the largest market in the Gulf, with estimates suggesting that the Kingdom imports 80 per cent of its needs. Viewed in relation to a market estimated to be in excess of $1.2 billion in 2005 this is a significant market opportunity. With a population growth rate hovering around 3 per cent per annum, current estimates predict a population of 30 million by 2008, and the demand for healthcare services is destined to increase.

According to a report from Euromonitor International, cough, cold and allergy (hay fever) remedies, analgesics, digestive remedies, medicated skin care, and vitamins

6

and dietary supplements were the main contributors to sales in 2005. Excluding NRT smoking cessation aids, which grew very well from a low base, vitamins and dietary supplements retained its position as the most dynamic sector in 2005, with sales growth exceeding 12 per cent. In addition to price increases, movements of shares in favour of highly priced multinational brands, new product launches (particularly in dietary supplements) and continued strong demand for many products like multivitamins calcium and vitamin C were the main reasons behind this performance.

Another report published in 2005 by the Gulf Organisation for Industry Consulting noted that Saudi Arabia was leading the GCC countries in the number of pharmaceutical factories (27) and the volume of investment in the industry (US$619 million). The Middle East presents tremendous opportunities for healthcare – per capita pharmaceutical expenditure was estimated to be about $58 in 2005, a figure that might seem insignificant when compared to $800 being spent in the US or the $350 in the UK, but the potential is obvious.

Safety and Security Equipment

Security concerns have prompted Saudi Arabia to focus on new areas of vulnerability in its internal and external security. On the safety side, the Government is also reviewing measures to tighten fire and safety regulations, which have not hitherto been rigorously enforced.

Although Saudi Arabia has a low crime rate compared to other countries, measures to check and curtail terrorist activities and the upgrading of security and safety systems has resulted in a growing demand for security equipment and services.

The government's privatisation plans should trigger considerable security upgrades within the electricity corporations and Saudi Telecommunications Company. Also with accession to the World Trade Organisation, new regulations are likely to give a further boost to the safety & security market.

A recent UKTI sector report listed the following items as being sought:

digital video surveillance with smart algorithms (artificial intelligence) with threat detection and counter terrorism analytical tools;

biometrics video surveillance technologies – face recognition, iris recognition; biometrics access control applications involving voice recognition, retina/iris scan, finger printing, hand geometry, etc., thermal imaging, night vision and video surveillance equipment;

road blocking equipment – bollards, rising kerbs, barrier systems;

vehicle/parking access control equipment – long range readers RF technology, OCR license plate recognition systems;

UVSS – under-vehicle video surveillance system (portable and fixed types);

weapons, drugs and other detectors and new cutting edge technology in security products and systems. Fire alarm, detection and prevention systems;

fire fighting and protection equipment, fire hose and reels, personal protection equipment and new technology/products relating to the fire and safety sector.

Telecommunications Equipment

The Saudi telecommunication market will continue to expand. The Saudi Telecommunications Company (STC) is already expanding the telecommunication network to double the size of the existing system. STC is expected to be evaluating and placing expansion projects for some years. The enhanced facilities will require the establishment of new telephone exchanges, replacement of old cables with fibre optic and the introduction of digital microwave systems. Local businessmen have taken to the mobile phone as though they were born to it, many changing their models with every new release.

Although the Communications and Information Technology Commission had previously stated that it would end the STC monopoly on fixed lines and would issue a new mobile licence by the end of 2006, these plans were still on hold in September 2006, with industry analysts suggesting that the changes could still be a year away.

6

Tourism

Statistics from NCCI show that around 3 million Saudi residents spend between SR 27-30 billion on vacations annually. The same source estimates that 24 per cent of Saudi families now engage in domestic tourism while 76 per cent engage in tourism abroad; 29 per cent in Arab countries and 47 per cent in non-Arab countries. Because the share of tourism in Arab countries is low in comparison, while expenditure in tourism abroad is higher, it is high priority for those interested in the economy of the Arab region to limit expenditure abroad. Experts in the travel industry estimate the average spending of an individual Saudi traveller at approx $2,000. In recent years there has been a dramatic shift in tourists destinations. In 2000 over 300,000 Saudis visited the US. Post 9/11 figures show that figure had dropped to below 80,000. With the average tourist reckoned to stay for 3 weeks and spend over $400 per day, that's a lot of money going elsewhere.

There has been little effort until recently to encourage any tourism apart from that generated by the annual pilgrimage to Makkah and Madinah. An estimated 3.5 million descend on the Kingdom each year to fulfil one of the requirements of the Islamic faith. Servicing pilgrim requirements is a major industry in the Holy Cities. Increasing emphasis has been placed in recent years to rounding up many of those who overstay and take casual (but illegal) work. With more pilgrims arriving and departing by air on organised tours, fewer of them are seen on the streets of Jeddah, the primary entry point into the Kingdom.

Tourist facilities have nonetheless been increasing rapidly, with the emphasis on resorts and amusement parks. Most of these resources are directed at encouraging Saudis and Arabs from adjacent countries to take their holiday inside the Kingdom. The Asir in the southwest, with its luxuriant green slopes in contrast to the many other arid areas of the Kingdom, is considered a prime region for such developments. According to HRH Prince Sultan bin Salman, the Secretary General of the Supreme Commission for Tourism (SCT), 'Morality is the basis of Saudi tourism and we will follow the teachings of Shariah while promoting this industry.'

The SCT is responsible for the national tourism development strategy, a comprehensive and strategic project for tourism development in the Kingdom. The strategy consists of three stages: assessing the general situation to develop the national tourism strategy for the next twenty years, putting the next Five Year Plans in place, and presenting a detailed strategic plan to develop tourism in order to build the local tourism industry. The first stage, the general strategy, has already been prepared and designed with continuous input and feedback from relevant public and private sector organization

There is a small but emerging market in catering for Western visitors who are prepared to spend time on a structured tour. Numbers are comparatively small but the market is definitely growing. See the Saudi Arabian Airline website for details of the type of tours on offer.

6

The Secretary General of the SCT, HRH Prince Sultan bin Salman bin Abdulaziz Al Saud was born in 1956. After completing his secondary education in Riyadh, he studied in the US, obtaining a Masters Degree in Social and Political Science. The Prince is also a qualified scuba diver and a qualified pilot and founded the Saudi Aviation Club in 2006. HRH is the Chairman of the Disabled Children's Association; co-founder of the Prince Salman Centre for Disability Research; founder and president of Al Turath, an organisation dedicated to the preservation and development of Saudi national heritage; a founding member of the Saudi Environment Society; Chairman of the Riyadh Science Foundation; a member of the executive committee of the Ar-Riyadh Development Authority and a board member of the King Abdulaziz Foundation Al Madinah Al Monawarah.

He is probably best known however for being the first Saudi astronaut, flying as a payload specialist on Discovery in 1985.

Training Services

Companies in the Kingdom are increasingly compelled to take on Saudis who are less able and often more expensive than expatriates. The answer to this problem is seen as better training and education. At present, the education system is failing to deliver enough suitably trained Saudis and cannot cope with the demands being placed upon it. There is an urgent need for economic

6

diversification to supply jobs for the thousands of young Saudis joining the workforce each year, who should be equipped and ready to compete in a market long accustomed to cheap foreign labour.

This process of Saudisation is dictating manpower training requirements. To enforce the government's stated desire to substitute foreign workers with Saudi nationals, a regulation was published in 1996 requiring companies with over 20 employees to include a minimum of five per cent Saudi nationals, and to increase the number of Saudi nationals by annual increments of five per cent. The Government has also ruled that non-Saudis may no longer hold certain jobs, and companies failing to comply with these regulations can be penalised. Mounting government pressure on the private sector to employ Saudis is forcing companies to recognise their own deficiencies and seek external assistance. However, many companies have built their businesses using comparatively cheap, yet often well qualified Eastern expatriates. Despite the regulations, if you speak about Saudisation to many business managers in the Kingdom, you will discover that they still face problems in actually finding Saudis who are willing to work at the market rates.

As companies attempt to replace trained expatriates with semi-trained or untrained Saudis, they find it increasingly necessary to provide training. A number of organisations, both Government and private, now offer business-related training courses, either in-house or at specialised institutions.

Many ready-made training courses from the West are incompatible with Saudi Arabian culture and must be adapted. The market is highly fragmented because of the need to cater for a variety of customer groups and the business opportunities are manifold and diverse. The market place is deemed to be highly competitive and extremely price conscious, although the quality of some of the available training remains a contentious issue.

Water Desalination Equipment

Saudi Arabia is now the world's largest producer of desalinated water with desalination meeting 70 per cent of the country's present drinking water requirement and supplying major urban and industrial centres through a network of water pipes covering more than 2,300 miles. Several new desalination plants are planned, or under construction, which will ultimately bring the final total to almost 30 such facilities.

The high population growth, increasing urbanisation, industrialisation and agricultural development, together with the climate increase the need for desalination. Since demand will undoubtedly continue to rise, this situation looks set to continue for the foreseeable future and Saudi Arabia will have to depend on desalination for many generations.

6

The Saudi Water Conversion Corporation (SWCC) is the only Government agency responsible for design, construction, operation and maintenance of desalination plants. Multi-flash stage and reverse osmosis systems are the most commonly used systems. Recently, the Government allowed private entities to establish desalination plants and the first was built by the Red Sea. This has created many business opportunities, especially for new technologies that can reduce the cost of producing fresh water, either in new projects or the updating of existing plants.

The Minister of Water and Electricity signed contracts worth more than SR709 million in November 2005 to establish six new water desalination plants. Speaking to reporters after the signing ceremony in Riyadh, the Minister said the new projects would double water supply in villages and towns on the Kingdom's west coast and end the water crisis there. The new plants in Al-Wajh, Amlaj, Laith, Qunfuda and Farasan would each supply additional 9,000 cubic meters of water daily, while the new Rabigh plant would pump 18,000 cubic meters of water daily. The Kingdom of Saudi Arabia launched the privatization of water desalination plants by awarding a SR9.1 billion contract to a consortium of Saudi and Malaysian companies in order to set up the third plant in Shuaiba, where the plant would supply 194 million gallons of water daily, as well as 900 megawatts of electricity. Work on the project will start 21 January and its first unit will begin production 13 October 2008. The Shuaiba-3, which is to supply water to Makkah, Jeddah, Taif and Baha, is one of the world's biggest co-generation projects for the production of water and electricity. In his remarks, the Minister added that the Kingdom would require SR350 billion in investment for water and sewage projects during the coming 20 years.

7

setting up a permanent operation

7 setting up a permanent operation

This section does not set itself up as the be-all and end-all reference for establishing an office. Its aim is to provide a sweeping overview for the visitor who is considering the possibility of a local office. The following pages highlight some of the pitfalls and benefits, give an insight into the legal situation, and run through some of the major issues to be considered, such as recruiting, finding premises, etc.

Overview

Saudi Arabia's accession to the World Trade Organisation has not, on the surface, made much of a difference to smaller companies wishing to set up trading operations in the Kingdom. The Negative List contained in the previous chapter still prohibits many foreign companies from engaging independently. Although the rules are changing, they favour the bigger ventures with large capital investment requirements. Non-Saudis are still not permitted to register as commercial agents.

The Saudi Government generally encourages direct foreign investment, particularly in the case of foreign investment in joint ventures with Saudi partners. Though Saudi Arabia technically allows wholly foreign-owned firms to operate, such ventures are still quite rare.

7

The Government and the private sector actively promote investment opportunities in Saudi Arabia, particularly partnerships with Saudi businessmen that expand job opportunities in the industrial sector that transfer technology to the Kingdom and expand Saudi Arabia's export capabilities. In general, any business that helps the Saudis diversify their economy or trains the growing work force is welcome, but foreign companies wishing to do business in the Kingdom are required to create a formal legal presence for themselves in one way or another. It is against the law for a foreign company to engage in business without a commercial registration.

Foreign investment

The increasing use of the Internet in Saudi Arabia, delayed until the end of the 1990s, is bringing new routes to the market for many companies. However, Saudi Arabia remains a market in which personal relationships are of critical importance in establishing good business relations. There are a number of options open to foreign firms, which dictate the procedures for establishing a presence in the Kingdom, depending on the type of business.

In theory, obtaining a business visa to visit Saudi Arabia can be done without any sponsorship by a Saudi national. According to the Ministry of Foreign Affairs, 'The Representatives of foreign companies are granted visas in their countries if the union and boards of industries and commerce make the request for the same.' A raft of relevant rules can be inspected on the website at www.mofa.gov.sa.

The Internet

In practice, foreign businessmen and investors (non-residents) who have been invited by Saudi companies and who have letters from their companies are allowed to obtain visas from their countries directly. In the UK more information may be obtained from the Saudi Embassy website at www.ukemb.mofa.gov.sa. Under the detailed rules and requirements for Business Visas the list of documentation in early 2007 still asked for a letter of invitation from a Saudi company along with the other documentation as described in Chapter 3.

Agents/Distributors

The appointment of a local agent or distributor is the most common procedure for companies wishing to enter the Saudi market, although there is no legal requirement to do so. Commercial regulations, however, restrict importing and direct commercial marketing within the Kingdom to Saudi nationals and wholly Saudi-owned companies. In addition, almost all Government purchasing is conducted by tender and, in the majority of cases, only Saudi companies will be invited or allowed to bid. Consequently, foreign firms may find it advantageous to establish local representation, especially for product lines requiring strong sales and service support. Foreign contractors wishing to bid for Government contracts must appoint a local service agent, and consultants must be represented by a Saudi consulting agency. Agent/distributor relations are governed by the Commercial Agency Regulations of the Kingdom of Saudi Arabia, and are administered by the Ministry of Commerce.

Keep in mind also that there are three major marketing regions in Saudi Arabia. The Western Region, with the commercial centre of Jeddah; the Central Region, where the capital city Riyadh is located; and the Eastern Province, where the oil and gas industry is most heavily concentrated. Each has a distinct business community and cultural flavour, and there are only a few truly 'national' companies dominant in more than one region. Many companies import goods solely for their own use or for direct sale to end-users, making the number and geographical pattern of retail outlets a significant factor. Foreign companies may find it useful to appoint different agents or distributors for each region with market potential. Multiple agencies and distributorships may also be appointed to handle diverse

7

product lines or services. Some companies, however, prefer to appoint a sole agent to avoid a conflict of interest particularly when bidding for Government contracts.

According to the Service Agency Regulations the compensation payable to a local service agent is limited to five per cent of the total contract price. However, many local agents may buy goods on their own behalf in order to sell them with a mark-up. That percentage is not always specified in advance. This may lead to disputes concerning the difference in sales volume between what the principle believes could be sold at his price and the amount an agent expects to handle at his price. Terminating an agent or distributor agreement can be difficult, even though Saudi policy has changed to permit registration of a new agreement over the objections of the existing distributor. Time is better spent in making the proper initial selection than in attempting to end an unsatisfactory relationship at a later date. The Saudi Arabian Ministry of Commerce can provide a standard format contract for guidance.

Branch Office

The establishment of a branch office is open to wholly-owned foreign companies only in certain circumstances. These include foreign defence contractors engaged in business with the Government. Approval for a branch office must be obtained from the Foreign Capital Investment Committee of the Ministry of Industry and Electricity, and a commercial registration with the Ministry of Commerce must be obtained once approval has been granted.

Branches thus established are normally granted a temporary commercial registration on the basis of a specific contract. Permanent commercial registration is only granted to companies deemed to have made a significant contribution to the development of the Kingdom and may require a significant capital investment. The prime advantage of a permanent, rather than a temporary, commercial registration is that once established, the branch office can engage in commercial activity in both public and private sectors.

Franchising

Franchising is a popular and growing approach for local firms to establish additional consumer-oriented business in

Saudi Arabia. Although the franchise market is small in relation to that in the United States or Europe, it is rapidly expanding in several business sectors. Apart from the highly visible fast-food franchise operations, which now have several local competitors, non-food franchises reportedly account for about 60 per cent of the franchise market.

Joint Ventures

These are usually set up as limited liability partnerships, which require minimum amounts of capital investment but cannot offer shares to the public. Less common, and requiring a much higher level of capital, is the joint stock company (JSC), which can offer shares. A JSC must have a minimum of five shareholders holding transferable shares. The minimum capital requirements are SR2 million for a private JSC and SR10 million for a public JSC. A joint venture in which each party to the venture holds title to his mutually agreed contribution is a third option. Foreign investment is regulated under the Foreign Capital Investment Law administered by the Ministry of Industry and Electricity (MIE), which must approve all investments except banks, which are licensed by the Ministry of Finance and National Economy. The Ministry of Petroleum and Mineral Resources handles investments involving mineral extraction.

Foreign investment was previously limited to joint ventures in which the Saudi partner holds at least a 25 per cent share, however rules designed to encourage foreign investment have set different limits depending upon the industry sector and in a few cases it is possible to set up a 100 per cent foreign owned company. There are no restrictions in the use of currency accounts or on the entry or repatriation of capital, profits, dividends, or salaries, provided tax requirements have been satisfied and clearance provided by the Department of Zakat and Income Tax. A number of incentives may be applicable, including a ten-year maximum exemption from corporate tax on the foreign investors share of profits, low cost financing, import duty exemptions and protective customs tariffs.

The procedure for establishing a joint venture varies depending on the type of operation. Within the MIE, the Industrial Licensing Department is responsible for evaluating and licensing industrial projects. External to the MIE, the Saudi Arabian Standards Organisation (SASO) may be involved to establish the appropriate standards for manufactured product; the Saudi Industrial Development Fund (SIDF) may be engaged to provide market research data or low cost financing; the Ministry of Labour and Social Affairs may be involved if foreign manpower is required; the General Organisation for Technical Education and Training may also get involved in training Saudis to work in the venture.

The website at www.sagia.gov.sa gives detailed lists of the appropriate rules, regulations and procedures for company formations, regulation of ownership and other business laws.

7

Investment Law

The new Foreign Investment Law allows international companies the possibility of 100 per cent ownership of projects. The law, passed in April 2000, gives international companies full ownership of the property required for the project or for housing company personnel, while enabling them to retain the same incentives given to national companies. The law permits foreigners to invest in all sectors of the economy, except for specific activities contained in a Negative List. Foreign investors are no longer required to take local partners and may own real estate for company activities. They can transfer money from their enterprises outside of the country and can sponsor their foreign employees.

In respect to the capital requirements, the minimum is SR100,000 for individual establishments, SR500,000 for companies, SR1 million for industrial projects and SR25 million for agricultural projects.

Liaison Office

Foreign companies which have multiple contracts with the Saudi government can establish their own liaison office by obtaining a Representative Office Licence from the Ministry of Commerce. Such offices are prohibited from engaging in direct or indirect commercial activity and are usually only permitted in order to facilitate co-ordination between the local and international activities of the company.

Under current arrangements the Liaison Office will have to furnish an annual statement detailing its activities and a set of accounts showing that the operation is entirely funded by the firm's overseas head office. The licence will also determine the maximum number of persons who may be employed under the particular arrangement.

Other considerations

Critical to determining the type of company or arrangement to enter into will be an understanding of the costs involved in operating in Saudi Arabia and how they may vary from those at home.

Salaries

Saudi law now requires that Companies with more than 20 employees must increase their Saudi workforce by 5 per cent each year, until the number of Saudis reaches 75 per cent of the total. In practice, however, authorities do not enforce the policy strictly, but examine the real intention of the companies concerned on a case-by-case basis. Despite this lenient approach, there are severe penalties for failure to observe requirements, and in failing to comply a company may be excluded from Government contracts and loans and may be refused visas and work permits for foreign staff. With increasing unemployment among young Saudis, the authorities are becoming stricter in applying these penalties, and non-Saudis cannot be hired for certain categories of employment, determined by the Ministry of Labour.

Companies may request a relaxation of the requirements if no Saudi nationals have the necessary skills and experience, but exemptions are rarely granted. The company must present a plan for future increases in the numbers of Saudi nationals in the company's workforce. In drafting an acceptable action plan, investors are encouraged to communicate directly with a Ministry of Labour officer at SAGIA.

Salaries for Western expatriates are generally not as high as they once were. As the Kingdom becomes less of a hardship posting, many Western expats work for little more than they would at home, treating the often short-term contract as an experience to add to their CVs. Companies wishing to attract a higher calibre of employee may still have to pay a considerable premium to secure the right man for the job. An employee's nationality and level of experience will have a large influence on the package offered, and the nature and location of the business will create variations in pay rates across the Kingdom. A typical manager's annual salary is around £40,000. Mid-level office workers are paid approximately £20-30,000 per annum. A clerical worker's base yearly salary is in the range of £8-10,000. A support worker (driver, caretaker) earns in the range of £5-6,000 per annum. However, there may well be more than just salary costs to consider.

It is customary to provide non-Saudi workers with furnished accommodation or a housing allowance as well as one or more return air fares to their country of origin on an annual basis. Expatriate managers may require married status contracts, which bring additional costs in transportation and housing costs for family members. Substantial add-on costs may also be incurred for families with children. If the children are brought to the Kingdom, school fees will have to be covered locally, if not, boarding school fees may be a consideration. Because women are not allowed to drive and restrictions apply to whom they may travel with, it may be necessary to consider employing a family driver for the school runs, shopping and social engagements. An extra vehicle may therefore be necessary.

Housing

Apart from those few situations where foreign owned companies may own property for use by their employees, non-Saudis are not permitted to own property and renting accommodation on an annual basis is the norm. Whilst a one bedroom apartment in town may be available for as little as £5,000 per year, most Western expatriates live in specially designed housing compounds where the rent and utility payments could be as much as £20,000 per annum for a 3-bedroom semi detached or £40,000 for a 4-bedroom detached family home. Most of the better compounds have swimming pools, sports and leisure facilities, cafés and restaurants, and often a mini-shopping mall. Standards vary considerably and prices in the market change so it is well worth finding out what other expatriates living in the territory consider acceptable. Rental agreements usually call for one year's rental to be paid in advance, often accompanied by a security deposit.

Recently, many senior expatriate employees who were prepared to work in the Kingdom themselves were not prepared to expose their families to the perceived security risks. In many situations, particularly those individuals working in the Eastern Province, have chosen to locate their families in nearby Bahrain, commuting on a daily or weekly basis. Dual housing costs in these situations may need to be considered allowing for batchelor accommodation near the workplace together with remote family accommodation.

Medical

Health insurance is now an essential part of a salary package. Whereas it used to be a discretionary item, in October 2005 the Cooperative Health Insurance Council (CHIC) imposed compulsory insurance on companies with more than 500 employees. By January 2006 this figure had reduced to 100 employees and during 2007 this should be extended to all employees. Where a company scheme does not exist, individuals are recommended to make their own arrangements. Where individuals have their own policies at home they should specifically establish their validity in the Kingdom. Companies are recommended to seek out internationally accredited companies with experience in the Kingdom who can assist in tailoring an appropriate package depending on the size and make up of the workforce.

Advertising and promotional expenses

Saudi Arabia is becoming an increasingly sophisticated market, but many of the business sectors in the Kingdom have no track record, nor have many industries faced the years of competition that have determined typical prices elsewhere in the world.

The costs of advertising in the media, be it in newspapers, trade magazines, on television or at exhibitions needs to be specifically addressed where relevant. Material may need to be prepared in more than one language or in a style in which your existing agency is unfamiliar. Advertising material relying on smart or clever use of one language may not translate appropriately into another. A household brand name in one country could sound like an obscene or inappropriate term when translated into Arabic. Computer programmes used to generate graphic material in the West may not be able to handle the Arabic script.

Restrictions may apply to the images that used to promote your product. Take fashion, for example; photographs of ladies wearing the sort of casual clothes seen elsewhere in the world are simply not permitted, and full body mannequins are not permissible in shops or stores. Alternative methods of presentation may have to be employed.

With food-stuffs, specific labelling requirements may dictate a packaging requirement unique to products sold in the Kingdom. Pharmaceuticals will require prior licensing, and some forms of machinery may not comply with local standards.

Take care, then, to consider the cost of every aspect of doing business in the Kingdom and make no assumptions based on experience gained elsewhere, however extensive that experience might be.

The clear message of this chapter is that each business situation is unique and those who are serious about establishing business in the Kingdom should seek professional and up-to-date advice before entering into any specific trading agreement. The Saudi Arabian General Investment Authority (SAGIA) has made major strides in improving the climate for foreign businesses to operate in the Kingdom and should be the first port of call for up-to-date information on all aspects of setting up an operation.

8

Riyadh

8 Riyadh

The nation's capital.

History

The capital city of Riyadh is located in the Central Province of Saudi Arabia in an area known as the Najd. This is considered to be the heartland of the country, It is also the most traditional and, in general, the most religiously conservative region of the country. Included in the region are a number of other important towns, north and west of the capital, such as Buraidah, Unaizah and Ha'il.

Though Riyadh is the capital of the country, it is only in since the 1980s that it has become the real centre of the Kingdom's government. Technically Riyadh was always the capital but until the early 1980s the ministries, embassies and virtually everything else were in Jeddah. They have now been moved to Riyadh and the embassies are all located in an area to the west of town known as the Diplomatic Quarter. Until the embassies moved to Riyadh, only the Kingdom's national airline was allowed to fly into the city. All that has now changed and many international carriers now serve Riyadh as well as Jeddah and Dhahran.

Najd ('highland') has never been easy to reach from the outside. The mountain barrier of the Hijaz towers above the land to the west, and on the other three sides lies a wilderness of sand..The region rises in places to 1,800 metres above sea level. The majority of business travellers to the city will arrive by plane and from the air the city's contrast to its surrounding environment is striking. Very little of what you see in Riyadh today is older than fifty years and a great deal is less than twenty. Most striking of all, to those who have come to know Riyadh, has been the pace at which growth has come to this small walled town and group of oases.

The history of Riyadh stretches back some two millennia. In pre-Islamic times, the settlement located at the site was known as Hajar. Irrigated by subterranean water running down from the wadis and the occasional rain shower, the collection of mud-brick houses in the town was surrounded by large date groves and fruit orchards.

In those times, one of the sights and sounds would have been the squeaking noise of wooden water wheels that worked around the clock to pump water from deep wells. Unlike some other oases where water would percolate to the surface in springs or artesian wells, Riyadh's water had to be brought to the surface from underground reservoirs

8

Riyadh City Centre

and then channelled through extensive waterways for the use of residents and the irrigation of trees. Whilst that system worked effectively for centuries when Riyadh was a small settlement, the rapid growth of the past half-century required new arrangements to supply larger quantities of water. Although five dams outside the city now collect what rainfall there is for urban use, most of Riyadh's water comes from pipelines that bring desalinated water from the Gulf city of Jubail; a waste water recycling plant supplies much of the irrigation requirement for public areas.

The modern name of Riyadh was originally applied to parts of the original town where date groves and gardens predominated. One of the few naturally fertile areas in the peninsula, the name derives from the plural of the Arabic *rowdhah*, meaning garden. For centuries, it was a green oasis in an arid landscape and accounts by travellers of past centuries invariably refer to the settlement's abundant water, describing the town as a vibrant centre of commerce with traders bringing their wares from all points of the compass.

8

The city has long since overrun the boundaries of the ancient mud-brick walls that once surrounded it and now stretches towards the horizon in an ever-expanding network of modern roads, high rise office blocks, residential suburbs and industrial parks. The architectural influences of the old walled city can be seen everywhere, particularly in the Qasr al Hokm District, which has been rejuvenated, as part of a multi-million-riyal project. Many traditional design elements are incorporated in modern government and commercial buildings as well as in homes and shopping centres.

Riyadh's modern history is closely associated with two specific dates, 1902 and 1932. The first being the year in which Abdul Aziz bin Abdul Rahman Al-Saud returned to the city of his birth, reclaimed the city and launched his three-decade endeavour to unify the tribes of the Arabian Peninsula; the second being the date that Abdul Aziz declared himself King and renamed his kingdom Saudi Arabia.

The recapture of Riyadh

The Riyadh of 1902 was no more than a mile across and consisted of the Musmak, the citadel that was also the seat of government, a large mosque, a spacious market place and several hundred houses, all built of mud-brick. A thick wall ranging as high as 8 metres surrounded the entire city. The city's famous date gardens were mainly located outside the walls. When Abdul Aziz returned with his raiding party from his exile in Kuwait he was able to enter the town surreptitiously at night to reconnoitre the town's defences. When dawn broke he and a small band of his followers were in position outside the Musmak gate to take the Rashidi governor and his party by surprise. The rest, as they say, is history and Saudi Arabia celebrated its centenary in 1999, it being 100 Hejira calendar years since this event.

8

On the 18th September 1932, the country's name was changed to the Kingdom of Saudi Arabia. The date marks the beginning of a period when the city was elevated to the status of capital of a nation covering most of the peninsula. The three intervening decades had been a period of slow but steady growth for the city. As King Abdul Aziz's realm expanded, so did Riyadh, slowly spilling beyond the city walls and into the surrounding desert. With the establishment of the modern Kingdom of Saudi Arabia in 1932, Riyadh's political and economic significance in the peninsula and the region grew immensely. Where for centuries the dominant features of the city and its size had remained largely unchanged, Riyadh now began a period of rapid expansion. As the seat of government of a young and dynamic country, Riyadh attracted more and more people who moved to the city to find employment, engage in commerce and generally help shape the new nation.

Expansion

During this period the steady population growth required a corresponding expansion of the city to accommodate the thousands of people who were settling in Riyadh each year. In the years immediately before the establishment of what we now regard as the modern Kingdom, Riyadh was estimated to cover about three square miles of land inhabited by some 30,000 people. Both the size of the city and the population grew exponentially over the following years. Within three decades, the population topped 200,000, reached 1.5 million by 1988, 2.5 million by 1994 and now at the dawn of a new millennium approaches, four million people. The city has steadily spread over the adjoining desert, growing tenfold within thirty years and becoming 200 times larger within sixty. Today, Riyadh covers an area of more than 600 square miles.

The City Today

Downtown Riyadh still has its maze of crowded streets and alleyways, but much redevelopment continues. Outside the old town streets are laid out American-style, in a grid system and navigation is a good deal easier. Major highways with three, four or even five lanes to each carriageway now ring the city extending into the desert at all points of the compass. During most of the day getting around this modern city is easy, particularly if you avoid a few well-known bottlenecks, one of the worst being the Khorais Road between 2 and 3 pm, when huge numbers of ministry workers head for home.

The unique agency that has helped make possible the planned expansion of the city is the **Arriyadh Development Authority's Urban Intelligence Service**. Using state-of-the art computer and telecommunications technologies, the service compiles and collates information on almost all aspects of urban life, analyses the data and offers it to government agencies and the private sector for planning future expansion. The data can be used for planning major projects, such as new roads, telephone networks or schools. It is also useful to a large firm planning a new outlet or an entrepreneur looking for the optimal site for opening a small business.

To develop the industrial sector, two industrial cities have been established outside Riyadh. Covering 5,300 acres of land, the two sites are designed to attract Saudi companies and joint ventures by easing the task of establishing new industrial units. Land can be leased at reasonable rates, and all utilities are available for immediate connection. Using data and studies provided by the Urban Intelligence Service and other specialised reports offered by the Arriyadh Development Authority, investors can pinpoint the need for specific products and rapidly establish a factory to meet demand in Riyadh and other cities in Saudi Arabia. As a result, more than 2,500 companies are currently involved in the manufacture of a wide range of consumer and industrial products.

In the capital of a nation that considers youth its most important resource, providing a first-rate educational system is a high priority on the national agenda. As the city has grown in the past half century, so has the

8

Commerce

Education

network of educational institutions available. Today, there are thousands of elementary, intermediate and high schools, plus two major universities and a large number of specialised colleges.

Health care

Likewise, Riyadh now boasts one of the most modern health care systems in the world. These include world-class hospitals, such as the King Fahd Medical City, the King Faisal Specialist Hospital & Research Centre and the King Khalid Eye Hospital, which are considered among the best in their fields. Hundreds of smaller hospitals and healthcare clinics are also scattered across the city.

To encourage young people to spend more of their leisure time in athletics and sports, the city has built many sports facilities. Some, such as the King Fahd International Stadium, are world-class complexes used for major events, but the vast majority are neighbourhood parks, playgrounds and football fields that are open to the public and much used by young sports enthusiasts. The International Stadium was inaugurated in March of 1988 and covers an area of half a million square metres to the north of the city. The translucent roof membrane forms a circle some 288 metres in diameter and is supported by 60 metre high vertical masts. Adjacent parking facilities can accommodate 26,500 vehicles.

Shopping

Riyadh's residents are keen shoppers, spending an estimated SR50 billion per year. Historically, the souks have been places to meet, shop or just pass the time with friends. Many traditional souks still exist in Riyadh and retain some of the flavour of the ancient bazaars, yet still manage to attract thousands of modern shoppers.

In Riyadh today, most of the shopping is done in modern malls similar to those found in any western city. In the spring of 2000 an estimated twenty new shopping centres and residential complexes are to be completed to serve the needs of this increasing population.

Two projects in particular dominate the Riyadh skyline; the **Faisaliyah Project** with a central tower exceeding 260 metres dwarfs the King Faisal Foundation building (60 metres) alongside. Investment in this multi-centre project was over $300 million.

The Kingdom Centre, a little further north along the highway is probably the tallest building in the Middle

8

East at about 300 metres (the height of the Eiffel Tower). Scheduled for completion in the year 2001, the tower provides over 10.6 square metres of floor space and is to be crowned with a vast sculpture incorporating a viewing gallery.

Arrival

The official history of Saudi Arabian Airlines, the national carrier, describes **King Khalid International Airport** (KKIA) as the world's most beautiful airport. It was opened in December 1983 and is referred to t as 'adhering to Islamic traditions' and 'harmonising with the natural beauty of the desert'. Even though the writers may have displayed an element of bias, there is no doubt that the building, inside and out, is indeed stunning.

The architectural splendour of the building does not, however, ease the rigours of modern-day travel. There are four separate areas, all interconnected; 'Royal', 'local', 'Saudia International' and 'Other Airlines International'. International passengers will find the beauty of the surroundings paling quickly into insignfiance when queuing for up to an hour to have passports inspected and, one hopes, stamped. After passing through passport control you will find yourself immediately beside the luggage conveyors where once again you may still have to wait for your luggage to arrive. Unfortunately the delay does not end when you collect your bags, because there is another queue.

Having recovered your bags from one conveyor, they now have to be loaded onto a smaller belt where you will be asked to open them for inspection. You will normally be asked to show your passport again and answer a few questions as to where you have come from, where you will be going and what you expect to do in Riyadh. On no account should you display any impatience or dissatisfaction. The inspecting officer is simply doing his duty. Answer briefly and politely and your passage to the world outside the airport concourse will be more smoothly effected.

Hotels

The airport is located about 30 kms to the north of the city and although there are plenty of taxicabs and limousines in attendance, most of the hotels will offer an airport collection service if arranged in advance. With the notable exception of the Sahara Hotel, which is located alongside the airport, most of the hotels used by business travellers are located within a few kilometres of each other. New arrivals will usually be met by their hosts. A taxi from the airport will cost about SR50-70.

8

Charity Dinner

In an unprecedented display of co-operation, Riyadh's top eight hotels pulled together at the end of 1999 to put on a Charity Dinner for the benefit of the victims of the Turkish earthquake disaster. Andrew Houghton, General Manager of Riyadh's Marriott Hotel who had previously worked in the region was able to call upon fellow Riyadh hoteliers from The Inter-Continental, the Hyatt Regency, the Sheraton, the Al Khozama, the Sahara, the Riyadh Palace and the Holiday Inn to stage an event attended by over 400 guests. Using their extensive connections through every level of Riyadh society, they were able to attract donations and assistance from companies and individuals too numerous to mention. All the hotels provided food, equipment and staff to stage the gala evening which was held in the garden of the Turkish Ambassador's residence. Entertainment was provided by an ex-pat band and local DJ and the event raised over $50,000 for the cause.

The non-availability of alcoholic drinks and the consequent absence of bars and clubs, mean that the hotels have to concentrate rather harder on providing dining or sporting options to attract their custom and this is where the differences between the hotels may dictate your choice. The following summary of top hotels in the city may assist in making your selection. Prices quoted are those given for single occupancy rooms for one night. Some of the executive charges actually include breakfast. All of the top Riyadh hotels offer excellent value for money in world terms and yet almost all will still offer a 'corporate discount rate' for regular or long-stay visitors and levy a 15 per cent service charge. When making a reservation always ask for a price 'after discount'. (Approximate $1 =SR3.745. £1 =SR6.15)

The Faisaliyyah Hotel ★★★★

This brand new hotel opened in the summer of 2000. It has luxurious rooms and generously-sized suites, all equipped with state of the art accessories. The Rosewood management is now in place, although not all facilities will be available before the end of the year. Restaurants include a 24-hour brasserie.
Standard rate: SR600; Suites: SR1,100
❏ Tel: +966 1 273 200 Fax: 273 2001

Email: alfaisaliah@rosewoodhotels.com

Riyadh Inter-Continental ★★★★★

270 rooms, 7 suites, 10 VIP villas, 16 cabanas, 2 restaurants.

More of a resort than a hotel, the Riyadh Inter-Continental sits in its own extensive grounds. Standard guestrooms have been newly refurbished and are well appointed with separated sleeping and working areas. The Executive wing remains popular and offers all the usual extras, including private lounge and inclusive additional services. Villas and cabanas in the grounds offer exceptional facilities if you have SR10, 000 a day to spend. Lots of recreational options including Riyadh's only in-town 9 hole par 3 golf course, 3 tennis and 2 squash courts plus some great dining options including the new Verandah Restaurant. Theatre-style meeting rooms for up to 1500, Business centre, Health club, 2 gyms, 2 saunas, indoor and outdoor pools, and bowling alley.

Standard room: SR 550; Executive Wing: SR 650
❏ Tel: +966 1 465 5000 Fax: +966 1 465 7833
Email: ruhha3@shaheer.net.sa

Hyatt Regency Riyadh ★★★★★

244 rooms and 73 suites, 4 restaurants

Downtown location on King Abdul Aziz Street (Old Airport Road) within range of commercial centres and ministries. Executive rooms include fax machines and satellite TV. Standard meeting rooms for up to 200 with a new wedding hall, which can accommodate 800. Business centre, fitness centre, sauna, squash and outdoor swimming pool. The Brasserie Restaurant serves breakfast in the morning and theme menus in the

8

evenings. Alternatively, there are excellent restaurants at the Shogun (Japanese) and Olivio's (Italian).

Standard room: SR550; Junior Executive suite: SR 1200
❏ Tel: +966 1479 1234 Fax: +966 1477 5373
Email: hyattriyadh@ruhrr.com

Riyadh Marriott Hotel ★★★★★

336 rooms and 35 suites, 2 restaurants

Well-placed just off the Khorais highway, on al-Mather Street offering easy access to key ministries, banks and commercial offices, a British general manager is on the bridge and the crew are well trained and responsive. The imposing atrium was renovated a few years ago and now contains a large seating area served by a coffee shop. All guestrooms are fitted with direct-dial phones and voice mail. The conference and banqueting facilities are elegant, but smaller than those of the nearby competitors. The al-Naseem restaurant offers a popular soup and salad lunch and theme nights. Conference rooms for up to 300, business centre, health club, sauna, massage, and pool.

Standard Room: SR495; Executive Floor: SR 525
❏ Tel: +966 1 477 9300 Fax: +966 1 477 9089
Email: marriott-ruh@prime.net.sa

Sheraton Riyadh Hotel and Towers ★★★★★

140 rooms, 30 suites, 12 villas, 2 restaurants

Entrance just off the junction of King Fahd Highway to the north of Olaya and close to the exhibition centre provides easy access to the diplomatic quarter in the west of town. This business-oriented property has 60 executive rooms, plus standard rooms complete with the usual extras. Dine on Middle Eastern, international and seafood specialities in the al-Bustan Restaurant or relax in the courtyard setting of La Piazza with Italian specialities from Tuscany.

The hotel has meeting rooms for up to 500, a businesscentre, fitness centre, sauna, steam room, pool, tennis courts and bowling alley.

Standard room: SR 450; Executive room: SR 550
❏ Tel: +966 1 454 3300 Fax: +966 1454 1889
Email: busctr@ogertel.com

The Al Khozama Hotel ★★★★★

175 rooms, 13 suites, 4 restaurants

Rosewood-managed, pleasantly appointed and well-stocked guest rooms with suites featuring extras like fax and modem connections, hi-fi system and safe. An American chef manages international, Italian and Arabian restaurants which come highly recommended and there are ample sports facilities.. It has meeting rooms for up to 600 and a separate auditorium for up to 400, business centre. fitness centre, indoor and outdoor swimming pools, tennis and squash courts.

Standard room: SR400; Suite SR750
❏ Tel: +966 1 465 4650 Fax: 966 1 464 8576
Email: snashar@kff.com

Al Mutlaq Hotel HHHH

163 rooms and 15 suites, 1 restaurant

This locally managed hotel lacks many of the facilities of the competition but the hotel attracts many Europeans with its no-nonsense pricing. Key features are a spacious lobby seating area and the al-Andalus restaurant which does a good seafood lunch on Thursdays. Opposite the Officers' Club on Old Airport Road a few minutes from the Khorais Road. Conference centre for up to 400.

Standard room: SR 350; Small suites: SR520; Large 2-bedroom suite: SR 900
❏ Tel: +966 1 476 0000 Fax: + 966 1 478 0696

Riyadh Palace Hotel ★★★★
270 rooms, 36 suites, 1 restaurant

Distinctive for its external architecture and located towards the centre on Prince Abdul Rahman Bin Abdul Aziz St. Guestrooms are spacious and comfortable. Le Café Blue serves as a lobby coffee shop and La Fontaine restaurant offers international and Arabic selections. Meeting rooms for up to 500, business centre, sports centre, outdoor pool, Jacuzzi, sauna, steam baths, spa, squash and billiards.

Standard rate SR 350; Junior suite rate SR520
❏ Tel:+966 1 405 4444 Fax: +966 1 405 3725
Email: ruh@riyadhpalacehotel.com

8

Minhal Holiday Inn Riyadh ★★★★

227 rooms, 15 suites, 2 restaurants

Located just off the junction of The Khorais Road (Highway) and Old Airport Road. The hotel has 50 executive rooms, complete with faxes, plus non-smoking options. Dining outlets include al-Yasmin, which offers a wide selection of international cuisine. Meeting rooms for up to 350, business centre, gym, outdoor pool, sauna and squash.

Standard rate: SR335; Executive rate: SR450
❑ Tel: 478 2500 Fax: 477 2819

Sahara Riyadh Airport Hotel ★★★★★

231 rooms and 16 suites, 2 restaurants

Comfortable deluxe hotel, alongside the airport with spacious luxurious guest rooms. Special rates apply to compensate for the extra travelling from this unique base. A wide range of international cuisine delivered on varying theme nights. Sales and Marketing Director Willie da Cunha can organise sightseeing visits to the desert or the city for individuals or parties.

Conference/meeting rooms for 500, business/secretarial services. Pool, tennis, health club, games room.

Standard room: SR 357 including service charges and breakfast;Junior suite: SR 552 inc. service and breakfast.
❑ Tel: +966 1 220 4500 Fax: + 966 1 220 4505

Restaurants

Riyadhis have been slower than their compatriots on the west coast in discovering the delights of eating out. But in recent years the number of independent restaurants opening in the city has rocketed. With so many bachelors in the city, some restaurants and cafés serve purely as feeding stations, while others attempt to recreate the ambience of locations far from Saudi Arabia. Not all have been successful and many fall by the wayside when they discover that the reality of catering for a fickle public is not all they thought it would be. The role of the restaurant reviewer, not an unpleasant one, has become almost a full time position.

Islam imposes some restrictions on dining out. Bachelors are separated from families and, in many places, unaccompanied women are not admitted even into the

8

family areas. Because unescorted women are not allowed in the company of men who are not their relatives, the dating game is severely restricted in the Kingdom and more than one establishment has been forced to close by authorities who felt that rules had been abused.

Restaurants and prayer times

Hotels have a dispensation when it comes to prayer time closure but independent street side restaurants have to close like all other shops and offices at the appointed times. This can catch diners by surprise when asked to leave the restaurant between courses or sit it out inside with all the lights off until the prayer time has finished. Even if you are inside, service will stop and staff may be seen peeping through curtains and shutters to establish if their actions are being observed by the religious police. Actual times vary daily but are published in the local papers and it becomes easier to avoid critical hours. It is generally westerners who find this most inconvenient since lives are not structured around prayer times in the same way as Muslims. Some restaurants do not open until after the last prayer of the day. Saudis generally would not go out to eat until much later in the evening, usually not before 9pm and occasionally after midnight.

8

Despite the restrictions, dining out is increasing in popularity. Fast food chains are cropping up all over the city with the international franchises (MacDonalds, Pizza Hut, KFC, etc.) having dozens of outlets. In competition, local chains have developed offering variations on the hamburgers and chicken that appear to be the Kingdom's staple diet.

The following review is not exhaustive, but contains only those establishments within the writer's personal experience. If you are seeking something else, Korean, Turkish, Moroccan for example, they are all available, take some local advice on what's still operating or what's new when you arrive.

Arabic
Baalbek
Prince Abdullah bin Abdul Aziz Rd
❏ Tel: +966 1 462 5734

Open now for more than five years, this restaurant offers fine, authentic Lebanese, Middle Eastern and continental food in a classy, comfortable atmosphere. The menu is complemented by mouth-watering daily specials. Take away or outside catering by arrangement has extended the appeal of this fine establishment.

Bourj Al Hammam
Takhassusi Street, opposite King Faisal Specialist Hospital
❑ Tel: +966 1 441 1401

Considered one of the best Lebanese restaurants in the Kingdom, the name means 'Tower of Pigeons', a reference to the house special – roast pigeon stuffed with rice. The interior is light and open with a Mediterranean feel. Leave some room for the magnificent baklava sweets.

Najd Village
Eastside of Takhassusi Road, a little south of the Euromarché complex.
❑ Tel: +966 1 464 6530

Bedouin-style dining inside a recreation of a Najd style house, where you can choose to sit on the floor if you wish. Carefully prepared traditional dishes with specialities like jareesh, qursan and marqooq are modestly priced and the kabsa, be it *hashi* (baby camel), lamb, chicken or shrimp, is well cooked and presented. An excellent introduction to genuine Saudi food.

Shaabiyah
Olaya Main Road, north of Arouba St junction.
❑ Tel: +966 1 465 8581

Authentic Saudi cuisine in a Najdi setting proffers all the Saudi specialities like Jereesh, kabsa, etc. The decor recreates a traditional courtyard through simulated mud construction with inlaid plasterwork and brass pots on the walls, white pillars and fountains. Air-conditioned dining tents outside of the main building offer an additional atmosphere for larger groups.

Yamal Asham
Olaya Main Road south west of the al-Akariah complex.
❑ Tel: +966 1 461 3292

Opened about 18 years ago, the original Yamal Asham, positioned itself firmly in the Arabic fast food market. It has quickly accelerated to become one of the most

8

successful restaurants in the capital city. An army of staff service the 3,000 customers that walk through the doors of this restaurant every day. Quick service and value-for-money are the trademarks, and traditional foods like *zattah* and *birak* are baked in ovens while you wait, whilst a range of other dishes are pre-prepared for you to make your selection. At the Olaya branch the ground floor is self-service (for men only) but there are single and family sections upstairs.

Chinese
Golden Palace
Mousa bin Nusair St, slightly east of the Olaya Main Road junction
❏ Tel: +966 1 465 7168

Innovative Chinese cuisine, prepared by Chinese/Indian chefs in a surreal setting where gurgling brooks meander among tiered booths. This ornate decor sets the tone for some ornate food presentations. An extensive list of delicacies from *dim sum* to sizzling meat platters. Great for late night dining.

Gulf Royal Chinese Restaurants
❏ Tel: +966 1 464 0121

At least two branches in the city including Olaya Road, behind the Cercon Buildings and King Fahd Road, opposite al-Arouba Plaza. Tanks filled with fish, not all of them destined for the table, greet you on arrival. Authentic Chinese decor of hand-carved ceiling panels and artwork. Typical of what westerners have come to accept as Chinese. Individual dining booths for groups of two to 20 provide a degree of privacy to enjoy the reasonably priced menu.

Hong Kong
West side of Olaya, south of the al-Khozama behind the SASCO filling station.
❏ Tel: +966 1 461 5513

A buffet menu on several evenings and lunchtimes offers exceptional value for about SR45. Chinese dishes include some excellent steamed dumplings and Peking duck, supplemented with some western style sweets.

Fish and Chips
Believe it or not there are two 'chippies' competing for

8

trade with this English favourite. The best is probably the one a few yards from the al-Nahdhad road junction with the Khorais Highway. The other (bachelors only) sits northside of the traffic lights half way along Tahlia Street. Eat in or take away, a large cod and chips will set you back about SR25.

French
L'écluse
Southside of Tahlia St, east of the now-closed Greenhouse supermarket.
❏ Tel: +966 1 465 7648

Essentially a French seafood restaurant, but with house specialities widening the style to include continental and Arabic favourites. An extensive selection of entrées compete for your attention alongside the main dishes of sole, salmon and sea bass. Freshly made desserts are almost edible works of art, try the 'Opera' cake if it's on. If you're undecided in your selection, leave it to Mohamed, the experienced Maitre d' to deliver a selection guaranteed to please. Both the singles section and the family area are beautifully appointed and can be carefully screened to accommodate parties of various sizes.

Café Can
❏ Tel: +966 1 465 8007

Another Tahlia Street outlet south of the old Greenhouse restaurant. The Café and the restaurant next door offer a full complement of quickies for those in a rush as well as more relaxed dining for that full blown three courser. Great coffee.

Indian
Makani
Northside of Thalateen St in Sulaimaniyah (not the one in Olaya). Just a small men only diner providing great Indian food and friendly service. Amazing how they can provide so much for so little outlay. Dinner for four for under SR100

Shezan
❏ Tel: +966 1 462 6608

Tucked between Olaya and the King Fahd Highway in the same region as many of the Chinese restaurants north of the computer souk. Mid priced and good value for money. Offers all the usual curries and biryanis but try the prawn jalfrezi for a hint of the Indian orient. Dinner for four cost about SR200 more if you choose the lobster.

Raj
❏ Tel: +966 1 461 0314

At the other end of the scale, Raj serves up authentic Indian food in a modern minimalist setting. Located in a quiet corner of the al-Bustan Centre on Takassussi Street. Dinner for four came to about SR450.

International

Al Bustan
❏ Tel: +966 1 454 3300

Main restaurant of the Sheraton Riyadh Hotel. Noted for rich, rotating international cuisine on theme nights. Saturday is steak night, Sunday is Chinese food, Monday Lebanese specialities, Tuesday Indian etc. A la carte dishes rival the generous buffets, the latter a hit for breakfast.

The Verandah
❏ Tel: +966 1 465 5000

The newest and best of the Riyadh Inter-Continental's offerings. Newly arrived executive chef Franz Thiess has taken over from Jean Luc Amman, the creator of this Californian-style eatery. Presentation is superb with many dishes including mouth-watering spices from the orient which create light yet satisfying fun-to-eat food. The atmosphere is a good as the food and the setting around the pool is quite simply superb. The décor from colourful crockery to comfortable chairs complement the fascinating combinations of fusion cuisine. Definitely on the 'best in town' list.

The Pavilion   ❏
Tel: +966 1 465 5000

Mainstay of the Riyadh Inter-Continental where buffets are the order of the day, every day. Help yourself from the generous display or ask the chef to create a dedicated dish at the live cooking station. Popular business venue for breakfast, lunch or dinner. Window views extend over the well-tended gardens. Chef Franz Thiess is also in charge here and is about to stamp his signature on all menus, so changes are afoot.

8

A locally produced restaurant guide, *Riyadh in Focus*, is available in most of the hotel bookshops. For a modest SR20, this pocket book will bring you up to date on eating out in the city and gives the telephone numbers for several hundred restaurants.

8

Steak House
Located on Thalateen St opposite and a touch west of the Azizia Panda supermarket.
❑ Tel: +966 1 464 9638

Established in 1992, this is a Western-style steak house, pure and simple. No frills dining on prime rib, T-bones and big cuts. Recommended for its lunchtime specials: sandwiches and all-you-can-eat deals of soup and salads for just 25SR. Great value, great food!

Italian
Olivio's
Up on the Fourth floor, at the Hyatt Regency on King Abdul Aziz Road
❑ Tel: +966 1 479 1234

Olivio's opened in late 1998, and has rapidly established itself as many Westerners' choice as the best in restaurant in town. Classic Italian design and an attractive piazza provide a stunning setting. Heinz Kohler, the Hyatt's head chef has created an inspired combination of enticing Mediterranean and Italian dishes to ensure that the Hyatt's strong reputation amongst diners continues. Service is impeccable: personal and attentive.

La Piazza
Newest offering from the Sheraton Hotel located on the ground floor
❑ Tel: +966 1 454 3300

Laid out like a village square in Tuscany, with quiet corners tucked behind a few pillars, clever lighting twinkles across the ceiling encouraging your imagination to escape from the harsh reality outside. Open only in the evenings, the locals are often seen queuing for a table, so reserve your spot early. The food is Tuscan style with an attractive array of antipasti, whilst the main courses delight. A very pleasant spot to spend an evening.

Da Pino
Al-Khozama Centre, 2nd level
❑ Tel: +966 1 465 4650

A modish, café atmosphere attracts a young Saudi professional crowd. Specialities include a delightful range of snack-like Italian pizzas, but other dishes are also worth exploring as a light lunch or evening bite. The al-Khozama Centre is an office /residential block just a few paces across the road from the al-Khozama Hotel

Scalini
❑ Tel: +966 1 481 0569

The unique location within the Diplomatic Quarter gives Scalini a distinct advantage in creating a restaurant with atmosphere. As you wait to order, tasty ciabatta-based snacks are offered; there is also a good antipasti selection. Over 20 pizzas vie for your attention amongst the freshly made pasta and meat dishes. Owned by Saud al-Shaya, who also owns a wholesale catering establishment, the food is fresh and the prices competitive.

Japanese
The Shogun
❑ Tel: +966 1 479 1234

Flagship of the Hyatt collection of restaurants, the Shogun offers the perfect spot for that 'power' dining lunch. Bills however come to match so be prepared for SR200 per head minimum. Top quality ingredients and skilled tepenyaki chefs prepare individual dishes in front of you and the experience is quite simply superb. A sushi bar alongside offers a snack alternative to the full-blown affair.

Furusato
❑ Tel: +966 1 465 7648

Located under the same roof as its partner restaurant L'écluse on Tahlia Street you may choose to select from both menus. Bachelors have three tepanyaki areas to sit in whilst families can be closeted behind curtains in a more private area. Sushi and sashimi are carefully prepared and presented. Alternative menus offer prices to suit your pocket.

8

Jeddah City Centre

9

Jeddah

Jeddah

History

Over 2000 years ago, Jeddah, half way down the Red Sea at a break in the coral reefs that run along the western seaboard, was a small fishing village. As the centuries passed it developed into a trading centre for merchants from India and travellers heading north from the southern highlands. The mountain barriers to the east channelled the ancient spice caravans along the coastal Tihama on their way to the Fertile Crescent in the north. Jeddah, Makkah and Medinah were towns along the route, which benefited from the traffic and even before the birth of Islam Jeddah was a gateway to the idol-worshipping pilgrimage centre of Makkah. After the historic cleansing of the Kabba, Makkah was adopted by the Caliph as the official destination for the Hajj (pilgrimage). This sojourn to the Holy City is considered the fifth Pillar of Islam, a duty every Muslim with sufficient means must carry out at least once in his life.

The Portuguese built the old city walls early in the sixteenth century but a short time later the town became home to the invading Ottoman Turks who controlled the region for over three hundred years. Jeddah's place in the history books is better documented from the start of the nineteenth century and its changing fortunes during the early period are fascinating.

In April 1803 Saud, the son of Abdul Aziz held siege on Jeddah for eleven days. Sharif Ghalib, leader of the tribes in the Western Province, withdrew to Jeddah. Despairing of ever being able to breach the walls, Saud and his forces eventually retreated to the northern deserts. One report from the time suggests that Sharif Ghaleb induced Saud to retreat after a payment of some fifty thousand dollars. By July of that year, Sharif Ghaleb had returned to Makkah and resumed government. Knowing he could not defend himself for any length of time a compromise was reached with Saud and Ghaleb was left in more favourable straights than many of the other regional chiefs.

By 1810 skirmishes in the Hijaz had rendered the land routes to Makkah uncertain. Ships from Jeddah were making regular trips to Suez, however, returning with cargos of corn and general provisions for the Sharif. Mohamed Ali the Pasha of Egypt resolved to despatch a flotilla of troops and provisions to restore Turkish

9

control over the region. In communication with Sharif Ghaleb, Mohamed Ali recognised the main sources of Ghaleb's income were the customs duties from the port of Jeddah and the Sharif's assistance was sought on the condition that this revenue would be left in his hands.

About two thousand men embarked at Suez destined for Yanbu and about eight hundred cavalry proceeded by land. Arriving late in 1811 the sea born invaders quickly assumed control over Yanbu and made contact with the land forces who had not encountered much resistance on route. At the time of the Turkish arrival, Ghaleb had meanwhile declined Saud's invitation to join him against the invaders on the grounds that he should garrison Jeddah in an attempt to forestall the recapture of Makkah. History does not say whether Ghaleb's plan was to fall in with the winner of the tussle or indeed attempt to drive both sides off after they had been weakened by the war. In January 1812 the Turkish troops advanced instead, towards Medinah where twelve hundred were killed on a single day. On hearing of the Turkish failure, Ghaleb at once fell in with Saud and succeeded in protecting his Jeddah revenues. Such was the changing fortune of the region that by November of 1812 Medinah had indeed fallen to the Turks with over a thousand of the inhabitants butchered in the streets.

Following the capture of Medinah another Turkish expedition of 1,000 mounted and 500 foot soldiers set off again for Jeddah and Makkah. On this occasion Sharif Ghaleb welcomed them in and joined the Turks with his own forces to attack and overrun Taif. Despite Turkish control over the major cities of the Hijaz, Saud supremacy over the region to the east was unbroken and Mohamed Ali thought it necessary to visit in person. Sending an advance of about 2,000 cavalry with 8,000 camels by land, Mohamed Ali and two thousand troops arrived in Jeddah in September of 1813. Sharif Ghaleb at once boarded the vessel before Mohamed Ali could land and once again succeeded in negotiating terms to retain exclusive rights over the customs revenues.

By now Jeddah had become a huge depository of provisions for the army and Mohamed Ali set about transporting supplies onwards to Makkah and Taif. This proved to be more difficult than it had previously seemed. The camels that had travelled through the Hijaz

Turkish invasion

had little or no food and soon perished. Within three months of their arrival in Jeddah their numbers had shrunk to about 500. Assistance from the Sharif was not forthcoming and very soon the pair were openly hostile towards one and other. Mohamed Ali contrived to kidnap Ghaleb who when threatened with beheading, in turn ordered his people to surrender to the Turks. Officers of the Pasha then set about an inventory of the Sharif's property, calculating his accumulated wealth at about £250,000. After a few days of captivity in Makkah, Ghaleb was despatched to Egypt with his family. Both he and reportedly all of his family died of a plague at Salonika in the summer of 1816. Jeddah's riches were once again in the hands of the Turks.

Later in the nineteenth century the opening up of the Suez route brought additional riches to the townspeople of Jeddah whose numbers had begun to grow. Jeddah fell to Abdul Aziz al-Saud in 1925 but the period of exponential growth did not occur until some years later. By 1945 the population was estimated at about 25,000 and by 1947 it was 30,000. By the early 1950s much of the city wall had been demolished as development spread to accommodate increasing numbers of settlers. During the 1960s and 70s the rise in the economic prosperity of Saudi Arabia directed even more of the rural population to the city where opportunities presented themselves more readily. By the 1990s, a figure of 1.5 million people is recorded and recent estimates suggest more than 2 million inhabitants.

Remarkable change and meteoric growth have therefore been the order of the day during the last twenty years and although many of the ancient dwellings were torn down as the city grew, the pace of destruction has eased with the preservation of historic sites now becoming an acceptable concern. The walls of the 1947 town encompassed an area of about one square kilometre; today, the city stretches over a distance of about 30 kms from north to south.

The City Today

As far as non-Muslims are concerned, Jeddah is the most important city of Saudi Arabia's western region. King Abdul Aziz and his troops took control of the city in 1925 and afterwards foreign representatives to his court lived in Jeddah rather than Riyadh. The embassies remained in Jeddah until the mid-1980s when they were all transferred to the Diplomatic Quarter in Riyadh. Nonetheless, there are still a large number of foreign consulates in Jeddah as the city retains its importance as the commercial capital of the Kingdom.

Climate

What will strike the visitor immediately on arrival is the climate. In summer and winter Jeddah is hot, but it is also humid. The hottest months are July and August when temperatures regularly reach 35°C (sometimes 45°C) with humidity often exceeding 90 per cent, particularly in September. Average temperatures are 23°C in January and 32°C in July. Some rain falls in the winter months but occasional storms may hit with serious effect at other times. The minimum temperature ever recorded in Jeddah was 9°C.

The main artery into the city from the north is the Medinah Road, a fast stretch of dual carriageway, which runs into the heart of the old city. Development in the north has been structured on the grid system and parallel roads chop up the city into easily navigable blocks. South of the east-west Falesteen Street (often called Palestine Road by the locals) which bisects the city about midway, development has not been so regular and although great lengths of asphalt carry huge volumes of traffic it is not always easy for a visitor to establish his whereabouts. In the heart of the old city, narrow alleyways and passages are thronged by the locals and the visitor would be best advised to avoid any attempt to use a car in this area.

No visit to Jeddah would be complete without a guided tour of the roundabouts and roadside monuments. Nearly every roundabout in Jeddah has a structure of wondrous design built on it, sometimes artistic, sometimes garish and sometimes just curious and whimsical. Michael Palin put the 'Bicycle' roundabout on the map when he encountered it his television series *Around the World in 80 Days*. Many of the roundabouts are lovingly maintained and sponsored by local companies. Those not to miss include the 'Aeroplane' roundabout which has an original Dakota mounted on white clouds, the enormous 'Boat' roundabout with several U-boats, the 'Hanging Lanterns' (pictured on the title page) which look better at night and the block of concrete with minis crashing into it. Along the famous

Monuments

9

Corniche is a wealth of examples of modern and traditional sculptures, refreshingly displayed for the benefit of all. Ask any local contact to take you on a tour and you will certainly find too many of these works of art to document.

Jeddah's Corniche is not just a huge open-air gallery. An imaginative blend of roads, pavements and gardens runs for over 20 miles along the coast to the west of the city providing a series of focal points for entertainment, dining out or simply meeting and walking with friends. Unfortunately in creating this man made testament to progress much of the coral reef previously enjoyed by the scuba diving fraternity has been completely and irrevocably destroyed. Where only twenty years ago the coral was reckoned to be the best in the world, divers plumbing the murky depths now encounter silt and rubble.

Away from nature's glories, modern day Jeddah is considered a shopper's paradise. There is an assortment of old fashioned souks selling incense and incense burners, jewellery, bronze and brassware, richly decorated daggers and swords, and huge brass-bonded chests. Bargaining is often expected, even for very modern goods such as cameras and electrical equipment. On-street parking is readily available outside all shops and virtually all car parks are free. In addition to the traditional souks there are over 75 modern shopping malls with almost every product known to man on sale.

Most of the older souks are centred around the downtown al-Balad area. **Gabel Street** is the main souk street of Jeddah, which leads to the treasures of the Gold Souk where gold is sold by weight with a small charge made for workmanship.

Through the underpass at the top of Gabel Street is an area almost untouched by the twenty-first century and traditional wares can be found here. Walk through this area if you have the time following winding alleyways that bring you to **Bab Sharif** with its many carpet shops, then east to **Bab Makkah** souk area with its spices and silks. Bab Sharif and Bab Makkah are the old gates of the city, which have been fully restored.

North Jeddah on the east of Prince Mitab Street and south of Tahlia Street is the **Syrian souk** known for eastern fashions, pots, pans and curtains, and off Sitteen

Street, past the old section of town is the **Afghan souk** where narrow roads of shops sell old and new high quality carpets and tribal rugs. Bargains are there to be had as well as memorable souvenirs. Other areas include the **Bawadi souk,** north of the satellite roundabout on Sitteen Street, which is a colourful souk with lots of children's clothes, luggage and perfume. **The Philippino souk** to the north of Saudia City is famous locally for quality copies from the Far East, fashions and luggage, especially polo shirts, watches and handbags.

Shopping

If you prefer to spend your time in more modern surroundings, the **Hera'a International Mall** at the intersection of Hera'a Street and Medinah Road has established itself as the most popular mall in Jeddah. Hera'a has undergone a vast expansion programme in the last year. Fine national and international shops mix in a modern upscale 112,000 sq.m. mall with family entertainment areas. Competition for parking near to the main entrances can be a problem at peak times in the evening.

Pilgrims

Jeddah is still the main point of entry for the millions of pilgrims who visit the Holy Cities each year. Although Jeddah is the largest commercial port on the Red Sea, most of the pilgrim traffic now arrives by air and it is the airport which is likely to be the first point of entry for the travelling businessman.

Arrival

King Abdul Aziz Airport borders the city to the north. Previously way out of town the developing city has crept across the desert to meet it. Jeddah airport is the largest, in terms of area, in the world. Amenities include a hotel, restaurants and plentiful duty-free shops where of course only non-prohibited items are sold. It has two main terminals (North and South) which operate like separate airports. The South Terminal is served only by Saudia and also operates domestic flights. The North Terminal, also known as the International Terminal, is served by all major airlines. Separate from the business traffic of the north terminals is an area known as the Hajj Terminal, reserved exclusively for the annual pilgrimage when over 2 million extra travellers descend upon the city. A smaller 'Royal' facility is also included within the boundaries. Travellers

KKIA

9

should note that only British Airways and Saudia fly in directly from London. Other airlines may well depart and end at the same point but always with a stop on route. The national carrier, Saudi Arabian Airlines, does not serve alcohol on any domestic or international route and other airlines which serve alcohol with meals will stop serving once over Saudi airspace.

Passing through passport control and customs can be time-consuming and travellers should be patient. Although things are improving and the average process time is 30 minutes, delays of two hours or more can occur, especially during the pilgrimage season when passenger numbers are swelled by 1.5 million. Although air-conditioned, the airport can be quite oppressive and it is recommended that passengers have bottled water with them except during Ramadan, when all eating and drinking in public is banned between sunrise and sunset. Airport toilet facilities are basic and passengers are advised to make use of the on-board aircraft facilities before disembarking!

9

All international passengers will have their luggage inspected by customs officials. Again, it pays to be helpful and patient: keep your passport handy and open all your cases and hand luggage for internal inspection. Magazines, videos and CDs may be retained for censorship and as this is time consuming it is advisable not to carry such items unless absolutely necessary. Carrying chocolates can also cause delays whilst the ingredient list is inspected for added alcohol. Do not attempt to bring liqueur chocolates into the country. Expect to be besieged by porters on clearing the formalities. Official porters are dressed in overalls and the airport authorities have recently set a standard rate of SR5 for a porter and trolley and SR1 for a trolley only. It has become customary in Saudi Arabia for anyone providing a service to seek extra payment as they are particularly poorly paid: this is left to the traveller's discretion.

When leaving the Kingdom a SR50 **Airport Departure Tax** now has to be paid. Introduced in 1999 this can catch travellers unaware and cause a last minute headache if you have already disposed of your local currency. Travellers must purchase a tax slip before departure and hand it in after passing through passport control. As with many new regulations in Saudi Arabia, the procedure for purchasing departure tax is likely to change and travellers should check with their hotel before leaving for the airport.

Hotels

Although stated elsewhere, it is worth repeating that all of the top hotels in Saudi Arabia offer excellent value for money in world terms and yet almost all will still offer a 'corporate discount rate' for regular or long-stay visitors. When making a reservation always ask for a price 'after discount'. Rates quoted are the standard ministry-approved rates and do not include the 15 per cent service charge. Businessmen coming in from outside may be able to take advantage of the lower rates offered to a local company if they do the booking for you. This may be as much as 30 per cent off the standard.

The following list is not exhaustive and new hotels are in their finishing stages at the time of going to press, and it is best to get up-to-the-minute local advice on which hotel would be more convenient for the offices you expect visit.

Jeddah Hilton ★★★★★

Currently under construction, the Jeddah Hilton promises to be an enormous and luxurious structure overlooking the Red Sea on the popular North Corniche. Opening date towards end 2000/beginning 2001. Plans are for 362 rooms, including 2 royal suites, 5 restaurants, business centre, health club and conference facilities for up to 2000 people.

Jeddah Inter-Continental ★★★★★

300 rooms (20 non-smoking), 36 suites, 24 apartments, 4 restaurants

Built in 1993, this vast business hotel is one of the city's most modern properties. Meeting rooms for up to 1,000, a business centre, health club, shopping arcade, outdoor pool, spa, jacuzzi, squash, games room, billiards and a beach club facility located 25 minutess from hotel are all available to residents. Situated a mile from the city centre on the trendy Corniche, guestrooms and suites all have balconies with sea views, while Club rooms offer the usual extras like in-room video and fax. Dining choices span Italian, seafood, international, Lebanese and teppanyaki, with the tea garden a leafy oasis and popular rendezvous. Superb facilities, great service.

Standard Room: SR 500; Executive Wing: SR 600
❏ Tel: +966 2 661 1800 Fax: 661 1145
Email: Jeddah@interconti.com
Website: www.interconti.com/saudi_arabia/jeddah

Crowne Plaza Jeddah ★★★★★

323 rooms, 53 suites, 60 furnished apartments, 4 restaurants

Superbly located on the Corniche in the elegant al-Hamra District, the Crowne Plaza is only 10 minutes from the city centre and 25 minutes from the airport. Several major shopping malls are within walking distance. The beautiful marbled lobby area reflects the superior Crowne Plaza status, which also ensures classy and comfortable executive bedrooms. The 60 furnished apartments offer a grand setting for the traveller, with full flexibility on length of stay. At over 1000 sq.m., the Crystal Ballroom is one of the most spacious in Jeddah. Food and beverage outlets include the popular al-Zahara (international), al-Yasmin Restaurant (Arabic) and Sakura (Japanese). Six high-tech meeting rooms, business centre, terminal for international airlines ticket reservation, free airport-hotel transfer, sports and health club with swimming pool, well-equipped gym, sauna and two squash courts, ample parking.

Standard Room: SR 460.
❏ Tel: +966 2 661 1000; fax: 660 6326

Holiday Inn Resort, Obhur ★★★★★

54 villas, 1 restaurant

If you are in a group or if cost is not a major consideration, consider one of the Holiday Inn's villas overlooking the Obhur Creek. Opened in 1997, this exclusive resort offers full air-conditioned villas with a large living room, fully equipped kitchen, private BBQ grills and dining room on the ground floor and 3 spacious bedrooms and two bathrooms on the first floor. Best of all, each villa has a spacious, private terrace with eye-catching views of the sea. Walk ten yards from your front door and you'll find yourself on the perfectly maintained beach, at 700 m the longest beach in Jeddah. If you don't fancy self-catering,

9

the restaurant offers delicious cuisine from a selection of Arabic and continental dishes with indoor and outdoor dining. Fully equipped conference room for up to 60 people. Gym, indoor and outdoors swimming pools, billiards room and beach volleyball. Jet skis, boats and bikes also available at extra charge. The Holiday Inn Resort is only ten minutes from the International Terminal and 30 minutes from downtown Jeddah.

Standard rate mid week: SR1,500 per night inclusive. Standard weekend: SR1,800 per night. Special offers often apply, for example 3 consecutive weekday nights at SR3,450 inclusive.

❏ Tel: +966 2 656 3030; fax: 656 1104

Hyatt Regency Jeddah ★★★★★

292 rooms, 38 suites, 4 restaurants

Blending Arab tradition with state-of-the-art services, this mid-town property with distinguishing *mashrabiya* window covers, provides easy access both to the north and to the south. Recent renovations at the Hyatt have seen the guestrooms, lobby, business centre and health club and Regency Club executive floors all given the treatment. Dine on reputable Japanese, Chinese, and continental cuisine or in the brand new al-Mashrabiya restaurant with its Arabic menu, show kitchen and wood-fired oven. Check out the roof top Shisha. Meeting rooms for up to 500 and a business centre. Gym, spa, indoor pool. Private beach club with diving facilities.

Standard room: SR 500; Executive wing SR 550 (inc. breakfast).
❏ Tel: +966 2 652 1234 Fax: 651 6260
Email: hyatt-regency-jeddah@jedrj.com
Website: www.hyatt.com/saudi_arabia/jeddah/hotels

Jeddah Marriott Hotel ★★★★★

156 rooms, 54 suites, 1 restaurant

Built in 1984 close to the site of the old airport and ten minutes away from the consulates and embassies, the Marriott had to rethink its strategy when the new airport opened a few years ago. One consequence of that has been its total renovation. Luxury rooms now offer voice mail and other executive extras. Some rooms are reserved for non-smokers. A business-oriented hotel, with the atmosphere of

9

a relaxed western tourist environment, the Marriott provides the businessman with a business centre, translation services, Internet access and an executive lounge. Car hire and chauffeur limousine services are provided by an in-house Avis desk. Impressive gift shop, oriental carpet shop and a barbershop complete the package. The al-Bassateen Restaurant serves international and Arabic cuisine while Le Bistro serves snacks in the lobby. Meeting rooms for up to 200. Pool, health club, sauna and steam room, games room, shopping arcade.

Standard room: SR 500; Executive wing SR 560
❏ Tel: +966 2 671 4000 Fax: +966 2 671 5990
Email: mhrs.jedsa.dom@marriott.com
Website: www.marriotthotels.com

Le Jeddah Meridien ★★★★★

254 rooms, 30 suites, 3 restaurants

Le Jeddah Meridien suffered an inauspicious start after its launch in 1998 with an unplanned closure due to unforeseen problems. The hotel re-opened part of its facilities at the end of 1999 but does not expect to be fully functional until the middle of 2000. Strategically located on the busy Medinah Road, Le Jeddah Meridien is next to the Jeddah International Market. Interesting pink architectural features complete with palm trees sprouting from the second floor. A business-oriented hotel, with voice mail and computer connections in all guestrooms. La Brasserie, a French style restaurant offers initial food-fare but additional restaurants are planned. Meeting rooms for up to 1,300 and business centre. Health club, sauna, jacuzzi and steam bath, pool, tennis, squash.

Standard room: SR 500; Executive Suite: SR 2,000; Diplomatic Suites: SR2,500
❏ Tel: +966 2 663 3333/6869
Fax: +996 2 663 2333/7748

Sheraton Jeddah Hotel and Villas ★★★★★

88 rooms, 34 suites, 8 apartments, 16 luxury villas, 17 resort chalets, 5 restaurants

Classically modern, blue-glass tower within a landscaped park on the North Corniche overlooking the Red Sea, 15 kms from the city centre. One of Sheraton's 'Luxury

9

Collection', it is beginning to look a touch worn these days, though a palm tree esplanade with majestic fountains makes a captivating entrance. Opulent guest rooms with balconies are a stylistic indulgence, butler service is available on the executive floor, and complete privacy is assured by 17 Sheraton Red Sea Resort villas. Ornately themed dining options include international, Chinese, Arabian and Indian cuisine. Much patronised by Saudis, government and royal household guests.

Meeting rooms for up to 450, business centre. Fitness centre, spa, pool, sauna, tennis, squash, private beach.

Standard room: SR 450; Deluxe room: SR 585
❏ Tel: +966 2 699 2212 Fax: +966 2 699 2660
Email: reservations_jeddah_saudi-arabia@ittsheraton.com
Website: www.luxurycollection.com-Jeddah

Alhamra Sofitel ★★★★★

253 rooms, 43 suites, 3 restaurants

Good central location near Dr. Sulaiman Fakeeh Hospital, 1 km east of US Consulate on Palestine Street and a recent refurbishment are combined here with a Gallic approach to presentation. It's stylish enough, although a little tired in places with marble and low-voltage lights in the lobby, and classically furnished, comfortable, spacious guestrooms. Best of 3 restaurants is the French Côte Jardin, while the Villa D'Aosta (Italian) and Sanabel (international menu and theme night buffets) are also popular. 5 meeting rooms and 2 banquet halls, fully equipped with OHPs, slide and LCD projectors, screens, TV/VCR, cordless microphones and podium. business centre. Health club, sauna, jacuzzi, steam bath, massage, pool, access to private beach nearby.

Standard room: SR 500
❏ Tel: +966 2 660 2000 Fax: +966 2660 4145
Email: h0824@accor-hotels.com
Website: www.sofitel.com

Jeddah Trident ★★★★

216 rooms, 2 restaurants

Further downtown than the competition near to the shopping areas of the Balad, the Industrial Zone and the Islamic Port. Service is a bit slack and simply furnished rooms have noisy air-conditioners. The Kandahar Indian diner is an Oberoi concept outlet, offering tandoori fare.

Meeting rooms for 350, business centre, health club, gym, sauna, steam room, massage, pool, Avis car rental desk and courier service available.

Standard room: SR 340; Deluxe room: SR 260 (The apparent discrepancy in the rates is explained by saying that the Standard rate may be subject to discount depending on the company booking whilst the Deluxe rate which includes breakfast is fixed).
❏ Tel: +966 2 647 4444 Fax: +966 2647 4040
Email: trhtljed@zajil.net

Albilad Hotel ★★★★

150 rooms, 38 bungalows, 3 restaurants + terrace

Charmingly landscaped and secluded setting for a well-equipped modern hotel set on the edge of the Red Sea, further down the Corniche and closer to the airport than its competitors. Dine on international cuisine at several inner eateries, or under the stars on the terrace. There is even a Mövenpick ice cream parlour. A good package at a competitive price, with bungalows an option for long stints. Excellent Friday brunch, popular with Western ex-patriates. Conference room seats up to 60 and there is one executive boardroom. A fully equipped business centre is due to open before the end of 2000. Fully equipped health club, jacuzzi, swimming pool, access to top-class private beach, tennis and squash courts complete the complimentary package. Airport shuttle service, courtesy transfer to downtown Jeddah, guided tours and boat tours also on offer. Flower shop, gift shop and barbers. Good friendly staff. Meeting rooms for up to 100 (and 500 poolside). Fitness centre, spa, pool, tennis, squash, private beach, horse-riding, bowling alley.

Standard Room SR 320; Double Room SR 420
❏ Tel: +966 2 654 4777 Fax: + 966 2 694 3737
Email: hotel@albmovenpick.com
Website: www.movenpick-hotels.com

Red Sea Palace Hotel Helnan ★★★★★

272 rooms and suites on 7 floors. No-smoking rooms available on request. 2 restaurants.

Now managed by a Scandinavian group the Red Sea Palace Hotel Helnan is affiliated to Helnan International Hotels. It is billed as the only deluxe hotel located in the

9

heart of downtown Jeddah that overlooks the Red Sea. It is close to leading business organisations, banks, travel agents, government offices, the old souk and modern shopping centres. Suites and guestrooms refurbished in 1999 are well equipped with satellite TV, safety features, and comfortable furniture. Meet and greet airport service, beach transfers, fitness centre, swimming pool, tennis court, city tours, extended 18:00 check out and ample free parking. Attempts to contact the Hotel regarding their rates and facilities revealed some shortcomings in their operational efficiency.

Standard room charges of SR450 were offered at a discounted SR270 inclusive!
❏ Tel: +966 2 642 8555 Fax: +966 2642 2395

Kaki Hotel ★★★★

218 rooms, 31 suites, restaurant and coffee shop

Newly renovated and air-conditioned rooms have vastly improved the basic value-for-money image of the Kaki Hotel. Rooms have balconies, music system, 20 satellite digital TV channels and mini-fridge. Complimentary services include free use of health club, sauna, gym and swimming pool, use of beach bungalows and transport to/from the airport, the beach and downtown shopping. A business centre, travel agent, barber shop, car rental counter and gift/book shop are also in situ. Four conference rooms each accommodate up to 100 people and 2 large halls are available for up to 1,000 people. The Sahara Restaurant is well known for quality Arabic/Chinese fare and the Nadwa Coffee Shop has an international flavour.

Standard room: SR345 inclusive;
Executive Suite 2 room: SR1080
❏ Tel: +966 2 631 2201 Fax: +966 2 631 1350
Email: kakihotel@icc.net.sa
Website: www.kakihotel.com.sa

Restaurants

Jeddah is overflowing with restaurants. Eating out is the main social activity and the alternatives are endless. Trends come and go, some restaurants may be more 'in', while others may go off the boil if key staff move on. Jeddah has its rich and its poor, and many of the imported labourers may not have any kitchen facilities at home. Some Indian or Pakistani 'soup kitchens' set up to cater for this army of expatriates offer an amazing variety of food for remarkably little money if you are brave enough to dive into the unknown.

Try the local street side *shawarma* if you fancy a little Arabic fare, variations on beef, lamb or chicken, with or without spices and pickles. They really are very good and only cost a few riyals. Fried chicken take-aways are everywhere and the local 'broast' is a pressure cooked variety which has a following of its own. The Al-Baik chain covers most of the city and meal of corn-on-the-cob, four pieces of chicken, fries, bread roll and drink will set you back about SR15.

Arabic

Al Rausheh Restaurant
Jeddah Inter-Continental
❑ Tel: +966 2 661 1800

9

Successful, traditionally bedecked Lebanese restaurant, serving extensive, good-value cuisine, especially the buffet on Thursday evenings. Mezze, houmous and moutabel, accompanied by those wonderful, crunchy mounds of fresh greens are the big draw. Open for dinner only.

Yasmin Arabic Restaurant
Al-Fau Holiday Inn Crowne Plaza
❑ Tel: +966 2 661 1000

Authentic Arabic fare and delightful decor – in the shape of an Arabic tent with brass lights and ornate woodwork screens. Daily buffets are a good place for a crash course in the local staples. Try the mezze selection, *shish taouk, kofta, couscous, om ali* and sweets, plus a selection of fresh seafood.

Yildizar
Off Andalus Street, behind Saab Showroom
❑ Tel: +966 2 653 1150

The most popular Lebanese eaterie in town. Ignore the plain decor – typical of village restaurants in Lebanon – because the food is seriously great, particularly the mezze and the garlic chicken. Service can be off-hand but don't be put off. A take-away-cum-snack area does brisk trade, too.

American
Happy Days Diner
Boksmati Centre, junction of Medinah Rd and Tahlia St

1950s American style diner. Great value for lunch but evenings in the family section can be noisy because of the games area for kids. Definitely a 'burger-orientated' State-side menu with Mexican sidelines.

Chinese
Gulf Royal Seafood Chinese Restaurant
Al-Andalus St, north of Tihama
❏ Tel: +966 2 667 4406

Part of the Gulf Royal chain of Chinese restaurants, trumpeting an extensive Chinese and Japanese menu of mostly seafood – over 75 dishes offered daily, including sea fish, prawns, lobster, shrimps and cuttlefish. The decor is vaguely oceanic (lots of wood and rope) but not especially effective.

Gulf Royal
Royal Crown, Prince Abdullah Street
❏ Tel: +966 2 665 3335

No expense was spared in the creation of the biggest Chinese restaurant in the Kingdom, opened in 1999. The food is to the usual high standard of the Lin family who now have five Gulf Royal Chinese locations in Jeddah

Wong Kung
Hyatt Regency Hotel
❏ Tel: +966 2 652 1234

Instantly visible from the lobby, the Wong Kung offers a comprehensive range of Szechuan, Cantonese and Hunan dishes prepared and traditionally presented. The surroundings are authentic Chinese, as are the teapots. Service and food commendable. Monthly promotions feature ingredients such as mango, ducklings and dim sum.

Xian Gong Sheraton
Jeddah Hotel and Villas
❏ Tel: +966 2 699 2212

Panoramic 11th-floor Chinese restaurant with views across the Red Sea. Appetisers include steamed dumplings, deep-fried prawn rolls or prawn toast, and Chinese soups. The main course entices with roast Peking duck with pancakes, fried whole fish with chilli paste, or lobster with garlic. Chinese traditional music adds to the pleasure of fine dining. The three chefs are from different regions of China, and the team is rotated every three years.

Fish and Chips
Harry Ramsden's
Corniche Road, south of the Intercontinental Hotel

Strange but true, well established now is a replica of the famous restaurant in Guiseley, Yorkshire. Offers excellent haddock and cod as well as local fish, with proper chips, mushy peas and a real cup of tea. Rumour has it that they are going to open a take-away on Tahlia Street.

French
La Cuisine
Palestine Street, opposite Jamjoom Centre
❑ Tel: +966 2 663 0363

Attracting lots of customers with its value-for-money French cuisine in a typical French bistro atmosphere. Service can be off-hand, but the food is first class. A pianist adds to the atmosphere in the evening.

La Nuit d'Or
Leylaty Ballrooms, al-Malek Road
❑ Tel: +966 2 683 3435 ext 180

A small step into the candlelit Nuit d'Or transports you to France and all that is admirable in Gallic cuisine, decor and ambience. The superb menu changes every month with daily specialities based on fresh fish from the market. Before or after dinner, guests sip tea in the club lounge, peruse books on the arts and enjoy the paintings. Exceptionally good value given the outstanding surroundings and service. No detail is missed. Subtle service is ideal for delicate business dinners.

Indian
Fawarah
Sheraton Jeddah Hotel and Villas
❑ Tel: +966 2 699 2212

Indian restaurant, open for lunch and dinner. Some of the mouthwatering dishes include Kashmiri salad, chicken tikka, chicken biryani, Kashmiri *pulav, nan bread, firnee* (sweet rice balls), *gajar* (carrot) *halwa*, and *masala chat*. Main courses are kept on warmers at the table. Elegant decor

9

features wicker chairs, Indian wall-hangings and screens, topped off by a marvellous blue and gold ceiling centrepiece.

Kandahar
Jeddah Trident Hotel
❏ Tel: +966 2 647 4444

The cuisine originates from the North-West Frontier region and the accent is on tandoori meat items. The ethnic tableware and moghul decor create a traditional setting for house specialities like butter chicken and chandni kebab. Interesting starters for dinner only include *aam ka ras* or mango juice, tandoori shrimp, *handi dum biryani*, *kulfi faluda* (ice cream), *chaat papri* and green salad. The décor and attention to the smallest details assure a complete dining experience in a traditional atmosphere. Authentic Indian food, scented towels, guests aprons, copper and silver traditional Indian tableware add to an extremely popular and good value restaurant.

Italian

La Fontana
Jeddah Inter-Continental Hotel
❏ Tel: +966 2 661 1800

Offers dining in palatial luxury for special occasions or important business dinners. Open every evening except Fridays from 1900-0100. Possibly the best Italian food in town. A distinctive and sophisticated atmosphere is created with original Italian furniture and a pianist entertains on Wednesday and Thursday. Portions are large so order selectively.

Il Castello
Off Khalid bin Waleed St, Sulaimaniyeh
❏ Tel: +966 2 665 2281

Described as the best pizza parlour in town by some. The vaguely Italian décor does its best but is distinctly tatty. Quick service and excellent value for money. Evenings are popular with families, when it can get very overcrowded.

Olives
Palestine Street, northside, east of Jamjoom Centre
❏ Tel: +966 2 661 0627

A Mediterranean restaurant, designed to transport you to the Med as soon as you enter from busy Palestine Street.

9

Well presented and interesting menu. Popular for important business dinners.

International

Al Diwan Café Restaurant
Hyatt Regency Hotel
❏ Tel: +966 2 652 1234

Very popular with the expatriate Arab community, this restaurant offers a comprehensive daily buffet lunch, including brunch on Fridays. Standard currency is Continental: salade niçoise, steak au poivre. In the evenings both à la carte and theme buffets come into play including international and Mongolian (Saturday), Mediterranean seafood (Monday), steak and lobsters (Tuesday) and Lebanese specialities

Al Ferdaus Restaurant
Jeddah Inter-Continental Hotel
❏ Tel: +966 2 661 1800

A regular haunt of visiting and resident businessmen alike, who enjoy the comprehensive lunchtime buffet in comfortable but not exceptional surroundings, as well as an à la carte menu. Specials include Navaratan korma, beef stroganoff and *khabsa* rice and meat feast. Theme nights are a big feature, but check out individual nights locally.

Boulevard Café
Al-Bilad Hotel
❏ Tel: +966 2 694 4777

Offers Caesar salad, US roast beef sandwiches and their well-known Chicken Gueggle, the famous dish from the heart of Switzerland. Quiet surroundings and open 18 hours a day.

Mövenpick Restaurant and La Terrace
Al-Bilad Hotel
❏ Tel: +966 2 694 4777

The main restaurant of the popular Al-Bilad hotel provides specialities from the Pacific rim: lava stone grilled meat and seafood dishes. Every evening there is a charcoal grill night at the Mediterranean Terrace, where guests select their favourite seafood or meat, charged according to weight. A large variety of excellent quality dishes from steak to lobster tail. Pleasant and comfortable surroundings. Excellent bakery on site.

9

Japanese
Hokkaido

Hyatt Regency Hotel
❑ Tel: +966 2 652 1234

This popular Japanese restaurant offers probably the best teppanyaki in Jeddah in traditional Japanese-style surroundings, complete with paper screens and excellent service. The restaurant also has a popular sushi bar. In the evenings during the business season (i.e. in the winter months) booking is recommended. Monthly specials include Japanese lunch boxes, tempura and sukiyaki.

Sakura

Crowne Plaza Jeddah
❑ Tel: +966 2 661 1000
Another popular Japanese restaurant known for its décor as well as its food. Principally a teppanyaki restaurant, there is also a sushi counter. A well-presented menu explains the Japanese terms clearly and includes an assortment of set menus combining soups, salads, sashimi and teppanyaki. Teppanyaki is expertly prepared in front of you .

Seafood
Fish Market Restaurant
Jeddah Inter-Continental Hotel
❑ Tel: +966 2 661 1800

An absolutely must for seafood lovers, with an outstanding view of the Red Sea and an amazing fountain. Visit the 'market' and select your order from the finest ingredients – you'll be given your own shopping basket. Well-trained chefs are on hand to advise. A perfect way to experiment with something new without committing to a plate full. Lunchtime buffets are excellent value.

Al Danah Restaurant
Near Sheraton Jeddah, north of Albilad Mövenpick
❑ Tel: +966 2 699 0090

On the Corniche, this seafood restaurant is made up of a series of glass cabanas jutting out over the Red Sea. It has as good a reputation for its ambience and vista as for its food, based on Indian, Arabic and Western cuisines. The Thursday night seafood barbeque is good value. Booking advisable, especially if a table over looking the sea is the choice.

9

10

Eastern Province

Eastern Province

History

The coastal strip bordering the Arabian Gulf, now known as the Eastern Province, includes the primary conurbation of Dammam, al-Khobar and Dhahran. Just north of Dhahran is Ras Tanura, the world's largest petroleum port close to Qatif and the new industrial city of Jubail about 80 kilometres away. To the south, the town of Hofuf lies at the centre of the al-Hasa Oasis.

Some archaeological evidence points to settlements in the Qatif area as far back as 3500 BC and early travellers referred to the Gulf as the Sea of Elcatif. Near Jubail lie additional ruins as yet inaccessible to the casual visitor, which may reveal even older relics. The al-Hasa Oasis is bounded by the al-Dahna desert and was at the centre of ancient trade routes which early traders followed to the Far East. However far back we investigate though, the truth is that most of the coastal settlements were no more than small fishing or pearling villages until the twentieth century. Indeed Dhahran barely existed until oil was discovered in the 1930s.

The three cities of al-Khobar, Dammam and Dhahran were once separate cities but have now grown to a point where they almost run into each other. Each area retains much of its separate character and some local administrative functions, however they are now effectively merged into one municipality known as the Dammam Area.

10

Dammam itself lies at the northern end of the group and is linked to al-Khobar by an expressway which takes about 20 minutes to drive if traffic is light. The Dammam Corniche overlooks the Gulf, while downtown Dammam, where many of the older companies have their offices, is concentrated in a small area on the southern perimeter. Dammam is an interesting place to wander through as there are many souk-like areas, whether it be gold, cloth or just vegetables. Al-Khobar is the newer, more modern part of the urban area, with another attractive Corniche. Dhahran grew out of the desert sands as a dormitory for the employees of Aramco and their families. Dhahran, originally 10 kms west of al-Khobar is the site of Saudi Aramco and the King Fahd University.

Dammam

Dammam is linked to the Central Province by major motorways and by Saudi Arabia's only modern rail

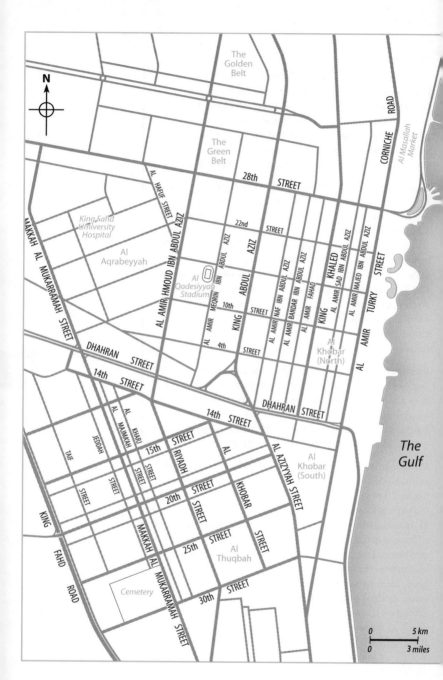

Al Khobar City Centre

track. Two or three trains make the 4-5 hour journey to Riyadh every day and pass through Abqaiq and Hofuf *en route* to the nation's capital. Hofuf, at the centre of a major date producing region, has a large souk and an old fort which add to the enjoyment of visiting this unusually (for Saudi) green area. The other major road in the area is the King Fahd Causeway linking Saudi Arabia and Bahrain. It is one of the most spectacular road construction projects ever undertaken. Completed in 1986 and known also as the 'Bahrain Causeway', the project was entirely funded by Saudi Arabia.

Growth in the region is inextricably linked to oil and its relevance to the region was first investigated in neighbouring Iran and Iraq where oil in commercial quantities was first extracted in the late 1920s. In 1923 Major Frank Holmes, a New Zealander acting on behalf of a British syndicate, gained an exclusive concession to explore for oil and other minerals in an area of more than 30,000 square miles. The syndicate was unable to persuade any oil company to invest in their venture and in 1928, King Abdul Aziz revoked the concession. After what must rank as one of the world's greatest lost opportunities, the Kingdom effectively broke the British monopoly of oil concessions in the Middle East and granted an oil concession to the California Arabian Standard Oil Company in 1933. In 1938 the vast extent of the oil reserves became apparent and the first barge of crude was exported to Bahrain. As oil production soared, so did the population and by the mid-1980s Dhahran began to resemble a small city, with tree-lined streets, neighbourhoods, public transport, hospitals schools and recreational facilities for adults and children.

Discovery of oil

10

According to a recent estimate, the Kingdom's recoverable oil reserves now represent about one quarter of the world's proven oil reserves. They also have about 5 per cent of the world's gas resources. It should be no surprise then to discover that the majority of business interest in the area is linked to petroleum and its derivatives. The modern industrial city of Jubail has been built to exploit the opportunity oil revenues have delivered and its success has actually reduced the Kingdom's reliance on those same revenues.

Oil today

Saudi Aramco now has the capacity to produce up to 10 million barrels of crude oil per day on a sustained basis.

It manufactures a wide range of petroleum products from oil and gas and markets those products both domestically and internationally. Now the world's largest oil producing company, it is also the Kingdom's largest employer outside the government, employing over 57,000 people. Over 75 per cent of the employees are Saudi citizens and their ongoing training, support and career development is a crucial part of the company activity. Companies, industries and individuals servicing Saudi Aramco's requirements make up a major part of the community in the Eastern Province.

In addition to the hydrocarbon related industries there are massive desalination projects in the region, which contribute to Saudi Arabia's position as the leader in the production of potable water from the sea. The volume of production allows the water from the Gulf to be piped to Riyadh over 500 kilometres away in the heartland of the peninsula.

No discussion of the area would be complete without mention of the 1991 Gulf War and the deliberate spillage of oil by the Iraqis that brought serious environmental damage to the region, although little evidence of the desecration remains today. The world's largest oil spill, estimated at as much as 8 million barrels, fouled gulf waters and the coastal areas of Kuwait, Iran, and much of Saudi Arabia's Gulf shoreline. In some of the sections of the Saudi coast that sustained the worst damage, sediments were found to contain 7 per cent oil. The shallow areas affected normally provide feeding grounds for birds, and feeding and nursery areas for fish and shrimp. Because the plants and animals of the sea floor are the basis of the food chain, damage to the shoreline has consequences for the whole shallow-water ecosystem, including the multimillion-dollar Saudi fisheries industry.

The spill had a severe impact on the coastal area surrounding Jubail. It threatened industrial facilities because seawater is used for the cooling system of primary industries and threatened the supply of potable water produced by seawater-fed desalination plants. Large numbers of marine birds, such as cormorants, grebes, and auks, were killed when their plumage was coated with oil. Beaches along the entire coastline were covered with oil and tar balls. The exploding and burning of approximately 700 oil wells in Kuwait also created

10

staggering levels of atmospheric pollution, spewed oily soot into the surrounding areas, and produced lakes of oil in the Kuwaiti desert equal in volume to twenty times the amount of oil that poured into the Gulf. The overall effects of the oil spill and the oil fires on marine life, human health, water quality and vegetation are immeasurable. To these two major sources of environmental damage, moreover, must be added large quantities of refuse, toxic materials, and 200 million litres of untreated sewage in sand pits left behind by coalition forces.

Saudi Aramco

Saudi Aramco is the multi-national conglomerate (fully Saudi-owned since 1974) charged with the exploitation of the Kingdom's massive hydrocarbon reserves. Today Saudi Aramco is a city in its own right, largely organised and populated by expatriates.

Due to the scale of its oil-related operations and of the whole infrastructure surrounding the city, Saudi Aramco is a prime target for businessmen aiming to supply services or products.

UK vendors wishing to sell to Saudi Aramco must first be registered as approved Aramco suppliers. This can be a lengthy process, however applications should be made to:

Aramco Overseas Company
Purchasing Agent
Schutterveld 14, 2316 ZB Leiden
PO Box 222, 2300 AE Leiden
The Netherlands

❏ Tel: +31 71 516 0600 Fax: +31 71 516 0610

Questions about manufacturer registration procedures should be addressed to:

Saudi Aramco's Vendor Liaison Unit
North Park 1
Room D-104
Dhahran 31311

❏ Tel: +966 3 00966 3 874 0004 Fax: +966 3 874 0312

Companies can also talk to Saudi Aramco's Materials Standardisation Division (MSD) in Dhahran and let

10

them know of any unique features of the product or application of new technology. MSD act as the technical procurement arm of Saudi Aramco's Purchasing Division and are responsible for the cataloguing of registered mechanical, electrical and pipe related supply items. An innovative or cost saving product may be approved by Aramco more quickly.

❑ Tel: +966 3 00966 3 874 0054 Fax: 00966 3 874 0568

After a product has been approved and registered by Aramco Overseas Company all necessary technical, financial and production information about the supplier is entered into the supplier Information System (SIS). In 1997 SIS held details of some 27,000 approved vendors worldwide. Of these, 3,000 were local vendors, 690 were local manufacturers and 8,000 were foreign vendors supplying through local agents.

Saudi Aramco gives sequential preference in placing orders to:

- Locally manufactured products
- Stocks of imported goods
- Products from foreign sources purchased from Saudi vendors
- Products purchased directly from out of Kingdom suppliers

If a foreign company is in a Saudi-based joint venture with a local partner, approval and registration is often faster. The product of a local joint venture is also more likely to be specified by Aramco as the standard when awarding future contracts.

For a new foreign supplier to the market, the quickest route may often be to enter into an agreement with a Saudi based approved supplier who will take stock in Kingdom.

Arrival

Many visitors to the Eastern province arrive by road, either from Riyadh after a 4-hour drive on a route now served by luxury coaches or over one of the many land borders on this side of the Kingdom. Most international travellers still arrive by air.

The King Fahd International Airport opened on the 28 November 1999. It covers an area of 780 sq. kms., making it the largest airport in the Kingdom. There are two parallel runways, each 4,000 m. long. The airport has the capacity to handle 7 million passengers annually and is approximately 70 kms north of Dammam and is now served by several highways. Flight time from the UK is about 6 hours 25 minutes. The airport is gradually introducing new shopping facilities as well as a number of restaurants. The coffee shop is modern, clean and the service is good. The airport is spacious, luxurious and with the exception of a few minor teething problems everything operates extremely well. Taxis wait outside the airport and a trip to al-Khobar will cost about SR70. A luxury limousine will cost about SR100

Exhibitions

If you're in the area for a while, why not take some time out to visit the Regional Museum of Archaeology and Ethnography. There's an interesting collection of local Bedouin crafts, traditional costumes and Islamic pottery, as well as some Stone Age tools.

Open Saturday-Wednesday, 0800-1430.
Admission free. 1st Street.

Worth a visit as well is the Aramco Exhibition Centre: A fascinating guide to the oil industry, explaining how the oil is brought up to the surface and how it is located in the first place. There are also displays on Arab science and technology.

Open Saturday-Wednesday, 0800-1830, Thurday, 0900-1200 and 1500-1830, Friday 1500-1830.
Thursday and Friday for families only. Admission free.

10

The new airport is unpopular with many of the local residents in al-Khobar. Although much smaller and less well equipped, the old airport could at least be reached in a few minutes from almost anywhere. Many of the regular travellers now choose instead to drive across the Causeway into Bahrain where they can relax or do a bit of shopping before flying out of Bahrain's international airport instead.

Saudi Arabian Basic Industries Corporation (SABIC)

The Saudi Arabian Basic Industries Corporation (SABIC) is an example of the practical results of the Kingdom's blend of long-range planning and long-term major investment drawing on public and private sources of finance.

SABIC was established by Royal Decree in 1976 – its task being to set up and operate hydrocarbon and mineral-based industries in the Kingdom. SABIC is the driving force in dyversifying downstream from crude oil exports and domestic refining, to exporting primary products (refined oil and gas products, fertilisers, etc.) and developing secondary industries (value-added petrochemical products, plastics, agrochemicals, etc.).

The Public Investment Fund provides long-term loans to SABIC on highly concessional terms. The balance of SABIC's capital requirements come from SABIC's joint venture partners. In addition, SABIC can make use of normal commercial loans. With these sources of finance, SABIC is able to undertake industrial projects considerably in excess of its own authorized capital of 10,000 million Saudi Riyals.

SABIC's Production

SABIC's Production by Product Group in thousand metric tons

Year	1990	1991	1992	1993	1994
Petrochemicals	7,669	7,620	8,880	9,491	11,268
Metals	1,786	1,766	2,148	2,553	2,383
Plastics	1,425	1,478	1,607	1,626	1,873
Fertilizer	2,186	2,280	3,045	3,443	3,683
TOTAL	13,066	13,144	15,680	17,113	19,207

(Source: Saudi Arabian Information Centre)

Shopping

The souks of Dammam are undoubtedly more interesting to the tourist, whereas the newer city of al-Khobar offers more in the way of convenience and modern facilities. The al-Rashid Mall is one of the largest shopping malls in Saudi Arabia with European stores such as Next, BHS, Oasis, etc. The shops open at 9.00 am every day except Friday and close around 11.30 at midday prayer time. They re-open between 3.30 and 4.00 pm closing at around 11 pm. On Fridays shops open in the afternoon at 4.00 pm. Shoppers familiar with Jeddah and Riyadh will find that in general everything starts and finishes a bit earlier on the east coast, largely because the sun rises earlier here. In addition to the shopping malls, the Alissa Souk in al-Khobar sells linen, shoes and computer software, King Khalid Street is famous for the gold shops and Prince Bader Street is good for ladies clothing.

Hotels

The choice of where to stay is more limited in the Eastern Province and those hotels patronised by western visitors enjoy a high rate of occupancy. There has been little hotel development in the Eastern Province in recent years. However, the Gulf Meridien Hotel has undergone a complete refurbishment to a very high standard, and is considered the best hotel in the area. What was the Oberoi Dammam Hotel is now the Sheraton Dammam Hotel and Towers, and on the Dammam highway the Carlton al-Moaibed Hotel is undergoing expansion. This refurbishment will provide a new health and gym centre for guests and residents of the al-Khobar and Dammam area. They are also adding self-catering villas for the business person who has a long stay in this region. Although not officially an hotel, a bachelor camp run by the Rezayat group occasionally has a few vacancies on its compound just off the Dammam highway and is worth checking out if you're in the region for a long stay. Chief among the attractions is the canteen on the compound, which is run by a British chef who knows how to feed someone away from home.

10

Le Gulf Meridien ★★★★★

329 rooms, 30 suites, 14 Villas 2 restaurants.

Considered the best hotel in the Eastern Province, all the rooms have a private balcony with views over the Gulf. A 300-space car park within the grounds is convenient for guests and visitors and other the facilities include an efficient business centre, several ball courts, a temperature controlled swimming pool and health club. Le Café de Paris offers a daily buffet and the highly regarded Lebanese restaurant is described as the jewel of the hotel. al-Nakhil, the coffee shop, serves up delicious french pastries in the cool, column-filled lobby which is one of the reasons making this a popular rendezvous. Overlooking a pleasant artificial promontory on the al-Khobar Corniche. No beach. Conference rooms for up to 400, (600 for a standing reception) business centre. Health club, swimming pool, billiards, squash, tennis.
❏ Tel: +966 3 864 6000 Fax: +966 3 894 1651
www.starwoodhotels.com/lemeridien

The Sheraton Hotel and Towers ★★★★★

300 rooms and suites 2 restaurants.

Friendly and helpful staff have assisted the changeover in ownership of this property which is now managed under the Starwood banner. New style of restaurants and refurbishment aplenty. The pick of the guestrooms have views over the Gulf from private terraces. There are popular sports facilities, but no beach. Convention centre for up to 1,000, business centre, health club, swimming pool, tennis, golf simulator.
❏ Tel: +966 3 834 5555 Fax: 834 9872
www.starwoodhotels.com/sheraton

Dhahran International Hotel ★★★★★

191 rooms, 2 restaurants.

Previously famous for its proximity to the airport and the number of famous people who walked through its doors, the hotel now has to compete on its own merits.

❏ Tel: +966 3 891 8555 Fax: 891 8559
Email: info@dhahotel.com.sa

10

Algosaibi Hotel

339 rooms and suites, 2 restaurants.

More Arabic than its main competitors this hotel is located eastside of the Dammam highway just north of Silver Towers. One of the few Saudi hotels with its own internet site where reservations can be made online. The Algosaibi is five minutes by courtesy bus to the town centre and has meeting and conference rooms large enough to handle 2,000 people. Gymnasium, Olympic size pool, tennis, bowling and indoor games room.
❏ Tel: +966 3 894 2466 Fax: +966 3894 7533
Email: reservations@algosaibi-hotel.com

Carlton Al Moaibed Hotel ★★★★★

161 rooms, 24 suites and 9 villas, 4 restaurants.

A business hotel conveniently situated near the Industrial City on the Damman-Khobar highway. Guestróoms are well appointed and the recently renovated 'Carlton Club' executive floor provides assistance for the business traveller. Conference facilities in the 1,200 theatre-style business centre. Health club, pool, tennis, snooker and billiards tables. Recently refurbishment
❏ Tel: +966 3 857 5455 Fax: +966 3 857 5443
Email: info@carlton-hotel.com.sa

Al Nimran Hotel ★★★★

116 rooms, 39 flats/suites, 2 restaurants.

Highlight at the al-Nimran is the new Latisia lobby café, with its pink marble floors and walls. A fashionable meeting place on Pepsi Cola Road, offering a wide range of beverages and excellent pastries from the Austrian chef. Recent up-grading has added some elegant new banqueting facilities for smaller parties with the Sara restaurant offering fine dining. Rooftop barbeques around the 'Skypool' are a novelty. Separate swimming times for men and women. Recent work has added better car parking. Centrally located between commercial and retail areas this is a good value 4-star hotel with comfortable guestrooms and a 'Brit' at the helm.

❏ Tel: +966 3 864 5618 Fax: +966 3 894 7876
Email: mail@alnimranhotel.com

10

Restaurants

The number and variety of establishments is undoubtedly growing, however the pace of expansion is slower than that of the capital Riyadh. Local residents will be able to tell you what is in current favour. Many of the restaurants in al-Khobar and Damman have high standards of cooking, but the ambience is lacking in many establishments because of the rules on segregation.

The Mishal Restaurant.
The Oasis Residential Resorts
❏ Tel: +966 3 887 1777

Spacious, sumptuous formal dining room designed primarily to serve the pampered expatriate residents of the aptly named Oasis compound, and one of the few places you'll find where mixed dining is permitted. Under these circumstances, by no means everyone is allowed in, but visiting Western businessmen should receive a warm welcome. Highlights of the ever-changing, French-inspired menu include lobster thermidor, baked stuffed prawns, and such desserts as *crème brûlé* and chocolate truffle.

Kodo Oasis Asian House Restaurant
The Oasis Residential Resorts.
❏ Tel: +966 3 887 1777

A Japanese restaurant in al-Khobar which actually benefits from the skills of a Japanese chef. Ample capacity dining rooms with opulent lacquered decor complete with the requisite suite of Samurai armour. Sushi bar, teppanyaki tables and tempura items provide a full range of options from this healthy cuisine.

Ristorante Casa Mia
The Oasis Residential Resorts.
❏ Tel: +966 3 887 1777

The third and perhaps most down-to-earth of the over-the-top Oasis compound's culinary triumvirate and certainly the most homely. Temptation comes in the form of grilled red peppers stuffed with anchovies in basil sauce, tortellini with salmon, spaghetti with forest mushrooms, five veal variations, plus steaks, lamb and pizzas. Popular for office outings.

Kyoto Japanese Restaurant Carlton Hotel

10

❏ Tel: +966 3 857 5455 ext. 5107

Relaxing atmosphere with a small Japanese garden and harmonious aquarium. Sushi bar and three teppanyaki tables.

The Dhow Restaurant
Dammam-al-Khobar Highway
❏ Tel: +966 3 882 5800

This amazing flying saucer-shaped cafe is especially popular with British expatriates due to the working-class English food. Includes excellent fish and chips, pies (with mushy peas), burgers, HP sauce and some barbecue specialities in the evenings. Good quick service.

Baba Habbas
Corniche al-Khobar
❏ Tel: +966 3 898 5971

The place to come for a class *shawarma*. It's one outlet of a very popular fast food chain serving a wide clientele from both the Middle East and Europe. Superb Middle Eastern dishes are allied to more Western offerings: the modus operandi is to choose both your ingredients and the way they are cooked. Seafood is particularly tasty and always fresh. The decor is functional but its setting on the Corniche compensates.

Le Soufflé/Pattis France
Corniche al-Khobar
❏ Tel: +966 3 898 3262

Recently modernised to allow clients to sit in or outside. Excellent French/Continental cuisine, washed down as always with only fruit juice or Perrier. Dishes range from Caesar salad and cream of lettuce soup to Dover sole, beef tenderloin and chicken *cordon bleu*. Run by a French chef, the ambience is as French as possible under the prevailing circumstances. The service is good.

Vienna Woods
Prince Bandar St
❏ Tel: +966 3 864 8257

Evoking the ambience of a Bavarian farmhouse, this unusual find is notable for the quality of its hearty

10

Austrian-Bavarian cooking. Wiener schnitzel, roast beef Rhine-style and sundry other veal and steak variations, many with homely brown sauces, should prove quite familiar to the British palate.

Grill: Chinese and Tandoori
7-8 Main Dhahran St
❑ Tel: +966 3 864 8865/894 3047

Well-established and deservedly well patronised for exquisite Chinese and Indian food, a happy atmosphere, and the chance to peer into one of the only open kitchens in the region. Reservations essential on weekends, short waiting, if any, on weekdays. A highly imitated concept, the original Grill is conspicuous by its nondescript signboard above white marble steps.

Gulf Royal Chinese
Corner of Prince Fawaz St
❑ Tel: +966 3 864 7898

One of a renowned chain of Chinese restaurants occupying the middle range. Good food, traditional ambience and Szechuan beef amongst the many specialities.

Mamma Mia
Al-Hamra Holiday Inn Hotel, Dammam
❑ Tel: +966 3 833 3444

Good homemade staples are the keynote at this, the first Italian restaurant in the Eastern Province, and now a notable stop on the local restaurant circuit. Best of a colourful menu are the appetising antipasti, spaghetti vongole, pollo cacciatore and the very special Pizza Mamma Mia. Clean and tidy with helpful staff.

Grill Room
Al-Hamra Holiday Inn Hotel, Dammam
❑ Tel: +966 3 833 3444

A range of steaks and other carnivore staples are the speciality at this cosy and unpretentious hotel-diner. Standout dishes include French onion soup, beef tenderloin and stroganoff, chicken and prawn curries, and a superb medallion of veal, stuffed with spinach. Attentive service does justice to the food.

10

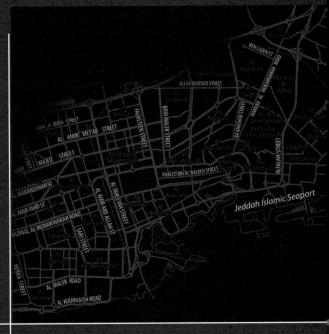

Appendix one: useful contacts

A1

Appendix one

Saudi Arabian Offices in the United Kingdom

Royal Embassy of Saudi Arabia
30 Charles Street, Mayfair
London W1X 8LP
t: +44 20 7917 3000   *f:* +44 20 7917 3255

Medical Section, Royal Embassy of Saudi Arabia
119 Harley Street, London W1
t: +44 20 7935 9931

Economic Section, Royal Embassy of Saudi Arabia
Liscartan House, 127 Sloane Street, London W1
t: +44 20 7730 8657

Saudi Arabian Cultural Office
29 Belgrave Square, London SW1
t: +44 20 7245 9944

Saudi Arabian Defence Office
22 Holland Park, London W11
t: +44 20 7221 7575

Saudi Arabian Information Office
18 Cavendish Square, London W1
t: +44 20 7629 8803

Saudi Arabian Airlines
171 Regent Street, London W1
t: +44 20 7995 7755

London Central Mosque
146 Park Road, London NW8
t: +44 20 7724 3363,   *f:* +44 20 7501 1111

A1

UK-based contacts

Trade Partners UK, Saudi Arabia Desk
Kingsgate House
66-74 Victoria Street
London, SW1E 6SW
t: +44 207 215 4839   *f:* +44 207 215 4831
www.tradepartners.gov.uk

Export Market Information Centre
Kingsgate House
66-74 Victoria Street
London SW1E 6SW
t: +44 20 7215 5444/5   *f:* +44 20 7215 4231
Email: EMIC@xpd£.dti.gov.uk
Website: www.brittrade.com/emic

Middle East Association
Bury House
33 Bury Street
St James's
London SW1Y 6AX
t: +44 20 7839 2137   *f:* +44 20 7839 6121
Email: mail@the-mea.demon.co.uk
Website: www.the-mea.co.uk

Arab British Chamber of Commerce
Belgrave Square
London SW1X 8PH
t: +44 20 7235 4363   *f:* +44 20 7245 6688
Email: bims@abccbims.force9.co.uk

The Saudi British Bank
18c Curzon Street
London W1
t: +44 20 7629 3709   *f:* +44 20 7629 5872

Saudi Arabian Embassies in Europe

Austria
Royal Embassy of Saudi Arabia
P.O. Box 126
Formanekgasse 38
A-1190 Vienna.
t: +43 1 362316

Belgium
Royal Embassy of Saudi Arabia
45, Avenue Franklin Roosevelt
1050 Brussels.
t: +32 2 6472492

Denmark
Royal Embassy of Saudi Arabia
Lille strandveg 27
2900 Helrup
Copenhagen
t: +45 31621200   *f:* +45 6472492

France
Royal Wmbassy of Saudi Arabia
5 Avenue Hoche
75008
Paris
t: +33 1 47660206,   *f:*+33 1 44402576

Germany
Royal Embassy of Saudi Arabia
Godesberger Allee 40-42
5300 Bonn 2.
t: +49 228 810900   *f:* +49 228 372068

Greece
Royal Embassy of Saudi Arabia
Athens - Paleo Psychio
71 Marathonodromou
154-52.
t: +30 1 6716911   *f:* +30 1 8479833

Italy
Royal Embassy of Saudi Arabia
9 Via G.B. Pergolesi
Rome.
t: +39 06 47660206   *f:* +39 06 48558658

The Netherlands
Royal Embassy of Saudi Arabia
Alexanderstraat 19
2514 JM
The Hague
t: +31 70 3614391   *f:* +31 70 3630348

Russia
Royal Embassy of Saudi Arabia
3rd, Neopalimovsky Per
4-Moscow.
t: +70 95 2453970   *f:* +70 95 2469471

A1

Spain
Royal Embassy of Saudi Arabia
Paseo de la Habana, 163
Madrid.
t: +34 91 341250   *f:* +34 91 340576

Sweden
Royal Embassy of Saudi Arabia
P.O. Box 26073
Skoldungagatan 5
S - 100 41 Stockholm.
t: +44 8 238800

Switzerland
Royal Embassy of Saudi Arabia
12 Kramburgstrasse
3006 Berne.
t: +41 31 3521555   *f:* +41 31 3514581

Saudi Embassies and Consulates in the U.S.

Royal Embassy of Saudi Arabia
601 New Hampshire Ave., N.W.
Washington, D.C. 20037
t: +1 202 333-2740   *f:* +1 202 944-3140

Saudi Consulate General in New York
866 United Nations Plaza
Suite 480
New York, NY 10017
t: +1 212 752-2740   *f:* +1 212 688-2719

Saudi Consulate General in Houston
One Westheimer Plaza
5718 Westheimer
Suite 1500
Houston, TX 77057
t: +1 713 785-5577   *f:* +1 713 785-1163

Saudi Consulate General in Los Angeles
Sawtelle Courtyard Building
2045 Sawtelle Blvd.
Los Angeles, CA 90025
t: +1 310 479-6000/914-9011   *f:* +1 310 479-2752

A1

US-Based Contacts

National U.S.-Arab Chamber of Commerce
1100 New York Ave., N.W.
East Tower, Suite 550
Washington, D.C. 20005
t: +1 202 289-5920   *f:* +1 202 289-5938

National U.S.-Arab Chamber of Commerce
135 S. LaSalle Street, Suite 1020
Chicago, IL 60603
t: +1 312 782-0320   *f:* +1 312 782-7379

U.S.-Arab Chamber of Commerce (Pacific) Inc.
PO Box 422218, San Francisco, CA 94142-2218
t: +1 415) 9200   *f:* +1 415 398-7111

U.S.-Arab Chamber of Commerce, Southwest Region
2711 LBJ Freeway, Suite 122
Dallas, TX 75234
t: +1 214 241-9999   *f:* +1 214 241-0114

U.S.-Arab Chamber of Commerce, Northeast Region
60 State Street, 20th Floor
Boston, MA 02109
t: +1 617 864-1432   *f:* +1 617 864-8448

U.S.-Arab Chamber of Commerce, Rocky Mountain
Region
6440 South Pontiac Ct.
Englewood, CO 80111
t: +1 303 694-9125   *f:* +1 303 770-9105

American Business Council of the Gulf Countries
(ABCGC)
c/o Intercom International Consultants
1101 30th Street, NW, Suite 500
Washington, D.C. 20007
t: +1 202 887-1887   *f:* +1 202 887-1888

U.S.-Saudi Arabian Business Council
1401 New York Ave., N.W., Suite 720
Washington, D.C. 20005
t: +1 202 638-1212   *f:* +1 202 638-2894

A1

U.S.-Saudi Arabian Joint Commission Program Office
1401 New York Ave., N.W., Suite 700
Washington, D.C. 20005
t: +1 202 879-4363   *f:* +1 202 638-1224

Chambers of Commerce in Saudi Arabia

Council of Saudi Chambers of Commerce and Industry
P.O. Box 16683
Riyadh 11474
t: +966 1 405-3200   *f:* +966 1 402-4747

Riyadh Chamber of Commerce and Industry
P.O. Box 596, Riyadh 11421
t: +966 1 404-0044   *f:* +966 1 402-1103

Jeddah Chamber of Commerce and Industry
P.O. Box 1264, Jeddah 21431
t: +966 2 651-5111   *f:* +966 2 651-7373

Chamber of Commerce and Industry for the Eastern
Province
P.O. Box 719, Dammam 31421
t: +966 3 857-1111   *f:* +966 3 857-0607

Banks in Saudi Arabia

Arab National Bank
P.O. Box 56921, Riyadh 11564
t: +966 1 402-9000   *f:* +966 1 403-0052

Saudi French Bank
P.O. Box 56006, Riyadh 11554
t: +966 1 404-2222   *f:* +966 1 404-2155

Saudi American Bank
P.O. Box 833, Riyadh 11421
t: +966 1 477-4770   *f:* +966 1 478-0823

Saudi Hollandi Bank
P.O. Box 1467, Riyadh 11431
t: +966 1 401-0288   *f:* +966 1 401-0968

A1

Saudi British Bank
P.O. Box 9084, Riyadh 11413
t: +966 1 405-0677   *f:* +966 1 405-0069

United Saudi Bank
P.O. Box 25895, Riyadh 11476
t: +966 1 478-4200/8075   *f:* +966 1 477-4469

Al-Rajhi Investment and Banking Corporation
P.O. Box 28, Riyadh 11411
t: +966 1 460-1000/2015   *f:* +966 1 460-2040

Riyad Bank
P.O. Box 22622, Riyadh 11416
t: +966 1 401-0908   *f:* +966 1 404-0090

The Saudi Investment Bank
P.O. Box 3533, Riyadh 11481
t: +966 1 477-8433   *f:* +966 1 478-1557

Bank Al-Jazira
P.O. Box 6277, Jeddah 21442
t: +966 2 651-8070   *f:* +966 2 653-0923

National Commercial Bank
P.O. Box 3555, Jeddah 21481
t: +966 2 644-6644   *f:* +966 2 643-7670

Islamic Development Bank
P.O. Box 5925, Jeddah 21432
t: +966 2 636-1400   *f:* +966 2 636-6871

A1

Ministries

Ministry of Agriculture and Water
P.O. Box 2639, Riyadh 11195
t: +966 1 401-2777/401 6666   *f:* +966 1 404-4592

Ministry of Commerce
P.O. Box 1774, Riyadh 11162
t: +966 1 401-2222   *f:* +966 1 402-6640

Ministry of Communications
P.O. Box 3813, Riyadh 11178
t: +966 1 404-3000   *f:* +966 1 403-1401

Ministry of Defence and Aviation
Riyadh 11165
t: +966 1 478-9000/441 6055   *f:* +966 1 406-2146

Ministry of Education
Riyadh 11148
t: +966 1 404-2888   *f:* +966 1 403-7229

Ministry of Finance and National Economy
P.O. Box 6902, Riyadh 11177
t: +966 1 405-0000   *f:* +966 1 405-9202

Ministry of Foreign Affairs
Riyadh 11124
t: +966 1 406-7777   *f:* +966 1 402-0100

Ministry of Health
P.O. Box 21217, Riyadh 11176
t: +966 1 401-2220   *f:* +966 1 402-6395

Ministry of Higher Education
Riyadh 11153
t: +966 1 441-5555   *f:* +966 1 441-9004

Ministry of Industry and Electricity
P.O. Box 5729, Riyadh 11127
t: +966 1 477-6666   *f:* +966 1 477-5488

Ministry of Information
P.O. Box 843, Riyadh 11161
t: +966 1 406-8888/401 4440   *f:* +966 1 405-0674

Ministry of Interior
P.O. Box 3743, Riyadh 11481
t: +966 1 401-1111   *f:* +966 1 403-3614

Ministry of Justice Ministry of Justice
University Street, Riyadh 11137
t:: +966 1 405-7777/405-5399

Ministry of Labour and Social Affairs
Riyadh 11157
t: +966 1 477-1480/477-8888   *f:* +966 1 477-2250

A1

Ministry of Municipalities and Rural Affairs
Riyadh 11136
t: +966 1 456-9999   *f:* +966 1 456-3196

Ministry of Petroleum and Mineral Resources
P.O. Box 247, Riyadh 11191
t: +966 1 478-7777/1133   *f:* +966 1 478-1980

Ministry of Pilgrimage Ministry of Pilgrimage
Omar Bin Al-Khatab Street, Riyadh 11183
t: +966 1 402-2200/402-2212   *f:* 402-2555

Ministry of Planning
P.O. Box 358, Riyadh 11183
t: +966 1 401-3333/1444   *f:* +966 1 401-0385

Ministry of Posts, Telephone and Telegraph
Riyadh 11112
t: +966 1 463-1152/4444   *f:* +966 1 463-7072

Ministry of Public Works and Housing
P.O. Box 56095, Riyadh 11151
t: +966 1 403 8888   *f:* +966 1 402-2723

Government Agencies

A1

Saudi Ports Authority
P.O. Box 5162, Riyadh 11188
t: +966 1 405-0005   *f:* +966 1 405-9974

General Organisation for Technical Education and
Vocational Training
P.O. Box 7823, Riyadh 11472
t: +966 1 405-2770   *f:* +966 1 406-5876

General Organisation for Grain Silos and Flour Mills
P.O. Box 3402, Riyadh 11471
t: +966 1 464-3500   *f:* +966 1 463-1943

King Abdul Aziz City for Science and Technology
P.O. Box 6086, Riyadh 11442
t: +966 1 488-3555   *f:* +966 1 488-3756

King Faisal Foundation
P.O. Box 352, Riyadh 11411
t: +966 1 465-2255   *f:* +966 1 465-652

Royal Commission for Jubail and Yanbu
P.O. Box 5864, Riyadh 11432
t: +966 1 479-4445   *f:* +966 1 477-5404

Saudi Basic Industries Corporation (SABIC)
P.O. Box 5101, Riyadh 11422
t: +966 1 401-2033   *f:* +966 1 401-3831

Saline Water Conversion Corporation (SWCC)
P.O. Box 5968, Riyadh 11432
t: +966 1 463-1111/0503   *f:* +966 1 463-1952

Saudi Arabian Monetary Agency (SAMA)
P.O. Box 2992, Riyadh 11461
t: +966 1 463-3000   *f:* +966 1 463-4262

Saudi Arabian National Guard (SANG)
Riyadh 11173
t: +966 1 491-2222   *f:* +966 1 491-4429

Saudi Arabian Public Transport Company (SAPTCO)
P.O. Box 10667, Riyadh 11443
t: +966 1 454-5000   *f:* +966 1 454-2100

Saudi Arabian Standards Organisation (SASO)
P.O. Box 3437, Riyadh 11471
t: +966 1 452-0000   *f:* +966 1 452-0086

Saudi Consolidated Electric Company, Central Province
(SCECO)
P.O. Box 57, Riyadh 11411
t: +966 1 403-1033   *f:* +966 1 405-1191

Saudi Consolidated Electric Company, Eastern Province
(SCECO)
P.O. Box 5190, Dammam 31422
t: +966 3 857-2300   *f:* +966 3 858-6060

Saudi Consolidated Electric Company, Southern Province
(SCECO)
P.O. Box 616, Abha
t: +966 7 227-1111   *f:* +966 7 227-1627

A1

Saudi Consolidated Electric Company, Western Province
(SCECO)
P.O. Box 9299, Jeddah 21413
t: +966 2 651-1008   *f:* +966 2 653-4139

Saudi Industrial Development Fund (SIDF)
P.O. Box 4143, Riyadh 11491
t: +966 1 477-4002   *f:* +966 1 479-0165

Saudi Arabian Airlines
P.O. Box 620, Jeddah 21421
t: +966 2 686-0000   *f:* +966 2 686-4552

Saudi Arabian Oil Company (Saudi Aramco)
P.O. Box 5000, Dhahran Airport 31311
t: +966 3 876-5229,   *f:* +966 3 876-6520

Presidency of Civil Aviation
P.O. Box 887, Jeddah 21421
t: +966 2 667-9000   *f:* +966 2 671-7376

Saudi Red Crescent Society
Riyadh 11129
t: +966 1 474-0925/0027   *f:* +966 1 474-0430

Central Department of Statistics
P.O. Box 3735, Riyadh 11118
t: +966 1 405-9638   *f:* +966 1 405-9493

Economic Offset Secretariat
P.O. Box 27040, Riyadh 11417
t: +966 1 478-4330   *f:* +966 1 478-4123

General Presidency for Youth Welfare Organisation
P.O. Box 7823, Riyadh 11421
t: +966 1 401-4576   *f:* +966 1 401-0376

Saudi Arabian Department of Customs
P.O. Box 3483, Riyadh 11471
t: +966 1 401-3334   *f:* +966 1 404-3412

A1

Hotels

Riyadh +966 1	tel	fax
al-Faisaliyyah		
al-Khozama	465 4650	464 8576
Hyatt	479 1234	477 5373
Inter-Continental	465 5000	465 7833
Marriott	477 9300	477 9089
Sahara Airport	220 4500	220 4505
Sheraton	454 3300	454 1889
Jeddah +966 2		
al-Bilad	694 4777	654 7098
Hyatt	652 1234	651 6260
Inter-Continental	661 1800	661 1145
Marriott	671 4000	671 5990
Sheraton	699 2212	699 2660
Eastern Province +966 3		
al-Nimran	864 5618	894 7876
Meridien	864 6000	898 1651
Sheraton	834 5555	891 5333

A1

Appendix two: the Arabic language

A2

Appendix two

Arabic Language

The Arabic language exists in its purist from in the words of the Quran, and this written Arabic, known as Classical Arabic (Fusha) has a much-studied structure and grammar, acknowledged by the Arabs themselves as highly complex. Mastery of classical Arabic is a highly respected skill.

Modern spoken Arabic, although building upon the principles of classical Arabic, has evolved into regional dialects, varying across the different parts of the Arab world but normally comprehensible to all.

The following are a few essential phrases of standard Gulf Arabic, and should help to get you through the courtesies.

Basic conventions

Arabic contains some consonants which do not exist in the Roman script, but can be approximated to the following sounds

Kha like 'ch' in the Scottish word *loch*
Gh like a rolled French 'r', sometimes described as akin to a gargle at the back of the throat
'ein A glottal stop, as in the cockney 'water', i.e. *wa'er*

Stressed syllables are marked in bold.

A2

A few basic phrases

Good morning	Sa**baah** al-**khair**
Reply (morning of light)	Sa**baah** an- **noor**
Good evening	Ma**saa** al-**khair**
Reply (evening of light)	Ma**saa** an-**noor**
Good night	**Tis**bah'ala **khair**
Greetings (peace be with you)	Assa**lam** a**lai**kum
Reply (peace be upon you too)	Wa a**lai**kum assa**lam**
Hello	**Mar**haba
How are you?	Kayf Ha**lak**? or **Kay**fak? (**kay**fik? to a woman)

Very well	Bikhayr (followed by)
Praise be to God	Al-hamdu lillah
Welcome (said by host)	Ahlan wa-sahlan
Reply	Ahlan bikum
God willing	Inshallah
(It is the convention to say this whenever referring to any future event)	
Goodbye (the one leaving)	Ma'a salama
Goodbye (the one remaining)	Fi iman allah

Making conversation

My name is Andrew	Ismi Andrew
And what is your name?	Waish Ismak?
Pleased to have met you	Fursa saeeda
(lit.' It was a fortunate chance')	
Honestly	Wallahi
(frequently used for emphasis)	
Do you speak English?	Int tatakalam Ingleesi?
I do not speak Arabic	La atakallum 'Arabi
I am American	Ana Amreeki
I am British	Ana Ingleesi
I am French	Ana Faransi
I am German	Ana Almaani
I am Swedish	Ana Suweidi
Please (general use)	Law samaht
Please (formal)	Min Fadlak (Min Fadhlik to a woman)
Thank you	Shukran
Thank you very much	Shukran jazeelan
Many thanks	Alf shoukr
Excuse me	Affwan
After you	Tafadhal (Taffadhali to a woman)
How?	Kayf?
How much?	Bikam?
How many?	Kam?
Who?	Meen?
What?	Aish?
What is this?	Aish Hadha?
What's the problem?	Aish al-mushkila?
There's no problem	Ma fi mushkila
What do you want?	Aish Tibgha?

A2

When?	Mata?
Where?	Wayn?
Why?	Laysh?
Here	Hina
There	Hinak
Is it possible?	Mumkin?
OK	Tamaam or Tayyib or Zayn
Yes	Na'am or Aiwa
No	La

Numbers

Zero	Sifir
One	Wahid
Two	Ithnayn
Three	Thalatha
Four	Arba'a
Five	Khamsa
Six	Sitta
Seven	Sab'a
Eight	Thamania
Nine	Tis'a
Ten	'Ashra
Eleven	Had-Ashr
Twelve	Itna-Ashr
Thirteen	Talat-Ashr
Fourteen	'Arbat-Ashr
Fifteen	Khamsat-Ashr
Sixteen	Sitta-Ashr
Seventeen	Saba'at-Ashr
Eighteen	Tamant- Ashr
Nineteen	Tisea'at-Ashr
Twenty	'Ashreen
Thirty	Talateen
Forty	Arbaean
Fifty	Khamseen
Sixty	Sitteen
Seventy	Saba'een
Eighty	Tamaneen
Ninety	Tiseen
One hundred	Maya
One thousand	Alf
Two thousand	Alfayn
Ten thousand	Ashrat alaaf

A2

One million	Malion
Billion	Miliar
Once	**Marra**
Twice	Marratayn
Three times	Talat marraat
First	**Awwal**
Second	**Thani**
Last	Akheer
Where is?	Ween?
Entrance	**Mad**khal
Grocery store	Ba**qa**la
Hospital	Mus**tash**fa
Library	**Mak**taba
Museum	**Mat**haf
Office	**Mak**tab
Chemist	Sai**da**liya
Police Station	**Mar**kaz as-**shour**ta
Post Office	**Mar**kaz al-bareed
Restaurant	**Mat**'am
Railway Station	Mahatat Qitar
How much is?	Bikam?
Do you have...?	Hal 'andak...?
Blouse	**Bloo**za
Dress	Fistan
Nightshirt	Qamees an-**nawm**
Shirt	Qamees
Shoes	**Jaz**ma
Long skirt	Tannoura
Socks	Sharab
Lipstick	Rouj
Perfume	**Riha**
Colours	
Black	Aswad
Blue	Azraq
Brown	Bunni
Green	Akhdar
Red	Ahmar
Yellow	Assfar
White	Abyad

Common adjectives

Large	Kabir
Long	Taweel
Small	Saghir
Short	Qasir

Negatives

I do not want	Ma abgha
I do not have	Ma 'andi
I don't know	Ma adri

Instructions

Look	Shoof
Give me	Ateeni
Go away	Ruh/Imshee
Hurry up	Bi sur'ah
Stop	Waqif
Never mind	La yahim or Ma yahim
Again	Marra Thaniah
Everything	Kull shai
All of us	Kulluna
Together	Ma'a ba'adh
Later	Ba'adayn

Time

Minute	Dageega
Hour	Sa'a
What time is it?	Kam essa'a?
It's two thirty	Essa'a ithnayn w'noss
Eight o'clock	Essa'a thamania
Quarter to ten	'Ashra illa rub'a
Quarter past three	Essa'a thalatha wa rub

Days

What day is it?	Waish al-yawm?
Monday	Yawm al-ithnayn
Tuesday	Yawm al-thalath
Wednesday	Yawm al-'arbi'a
Thursday	Yawm al-khamis
Friday	Yawm al-juma'a
Saturday	Yawm as-sabt
Sunday	Yawm al-ahad

A2

Money

Where can I change some money?	Wayn aghayir al-'umla?
There at the Bank	Hinaak fil **bank**
Is there a bank at the airport?	Fi **bank** fil matar?
Yes, over there	Naam, **huwa** hinaak

Accommodation

Hotel	Funduk
I have a reservation for one room	'Andi hajz li ghurfa wahida
I need a quiet room	Abga ghurfa hadiya
I need the room for two days	Abga al-ghurfa li yawmayn.
I need the room for one week	Abga al-ghurfa li usbu'ah
Single or double bed?	Bi-sareer wahad aw sareerayn?
Room with a double bed, please	Ghorfa bi sirareerayn law samaht
How much per night?	Kam sir'a li laila?
OK that's fine	Tayyib, hedha zein
May I have the bill	Al-fatoora law samaht
Thank you for the good service	Shukran lil khidma al-mumtaaza

Food

Restaurant	mat'an
What would you like to eat?	Waish tibgha takul?
Would you please bring some,	Law samaht jiblee..
The menu	Wajbah
Bananas .	Mooz
Bread	Khobz or Aish
Butter	Zibda
Chicken	Dajaj
Coffee	Gahwa
Corn	Dhurrah
Cucumber	Khiyar
Dates	Tamar
Garlic	Toum
Grapes	'ainab
Lamb	Laham kharoof
Lettuce	Khass
Fresh milk	Haleeb
Olives	Zaytoun

A2

Onions	**Basal**
Rice	Ruzz
Roast Beef	**Laham mash**wee
Salt	Milh
Soup	**Shorba**
Steak	Steak
Sugar	**Sukkar**
Tomatoes	Tamatim
Vegetables	**Khudaar**
Vinegar	Khall
Water	**Maiya**

A2

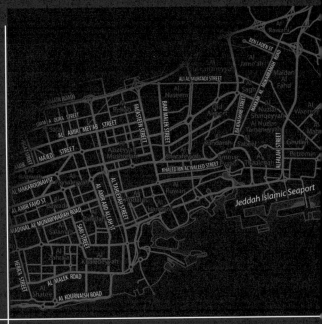

Appendix three: commercial support for US companies

A3

Appendix three

Directory of Export Assistance Centers

Cities in capital letters are centres which combine the export promotion and trade finance service of the Department of Commerce, the Export-Import Bank, the Small Business Administration and the Agency of International Development. (All numbers prefixed +1)

ALABAMA
Birmingham, Alabama - George Norton, Director
950 22nd Street North, Room 707, ZIP 35203
t: : (205) 731-1331   *f:* (205) 731-0076

ALASKA
Anchorage, Alaska - Charles Becker, Director
550 West 7th Ave., Suite 1770, ZIP: 99501
t: (907) 271-6237   *f:* (907) 271-6242

ARIZONA
Phoenix, Arizona - Frank Woods, Director
2901 N. Central Ave., Suite 970, ZIP 85012
t: (602) 640-2513   *f:* (602) 640-2518

CALIFORNIA - LONG BEACH
Joseph F Sachs, Director
Mary Delmege, CS Director
One World Trade Center, Ste. 1670, ZIP: 90831
t: (562) 980-4550   *f:* (562) 980-4561

CALIFORNIA - SAN JOSE
101 Park Center Plaza, Ste. 1001, ZIP: 95113
t: (408) 271-7300   *f:* (408) 271-7307

COLORADO - DENVER
Nancy Charles-Parker, Director
1625 Broadway, Suite 680, ZIP: 80202
t: (303) 844-6623   *f:* (303) 844-5651

A3

CONNECTICUT
Middletown, Connecticut - Carl Jacobsen, Director
213 Court Street, Suite 903 ZIP: 06457-3346
t: (860) 638-6950   *f:* (860) 638-6970

DELAWARE
Served by the Philadelphia, Pennsylvania U.S. Export
AssistanceCenter

FLORIDA - MIAMI
John McCartney, Director
P.O. Box 590570, ZIP: 33159
5600 Northwest 36th St., Ste. 617, ZIP: 33166
t: (305) 526-7425   *f:* (305) 526-7434

GEORGIA - ATLANTA
Samuel Troy, Director
285 Peachtree Center Avenue, NE, Suite 200
ZIP: 30303-1229
t: (404) 657-1900   *f:* (404) 657-1970

HAWAII
Honolulu, Hawaii - Greg Wong, Manager
1001 Bishop St.; Pacific Tower; Suite 1140
ZIP: 96813
t: (808) 522-8040   *f:* (808) 522-8045

IDAHO
Boise, Idaho - James Hellwig, Manager
700 West State Street, 2nd Floor, ZIP: 83720
t: (208) 334-3857   *f:* (208) 334-2783

ILLINOIS - CHICAGO
Mary Joyce, Director
55 West Monroe Street, Suite 2440, ZIP: 60603
t: (312) 353-8045   *f:* (312) 353-8120

A3

INDIANA

Indianapolis, Indiana - Dan Swart, Manager
11405 N. Pennsylvania Street, Suite 106
Carmel, IN, ZIP: 46032
t: (317) 582-2300   *f:* (317) 582-2301

IOWA

Des Moines, Iowa - Allen Patch, Director
601 Locust Street, Suite 100, ZIP: 50309-3739
t: (515) 288-8614   *f:* (515) 288-1437

KANSAS

Wichita, Kansas - George D. Lavid, Manager
209 East William, Suite 300, ZIP: 67202-4001
t: (316) 269-6160   *f:* (316) 269-6111

KENTUCKY

Louisville, Kentucky - John Autin, Director
601 W. Broadway, Room 634B , ZIP: 40202
t: (502) 582-5066   *f:* (502) 582-6573

LOUISIANA - DELTA

Patricia Holt, Acting Director
365 Canal Street, Suite 1170
New Orleans ZIP: 70130
t: (504) 589-6546   *f:* (504) 589-2337

MAINE

Portland, Maine - Jeffrey Porter, Manager
c/o Maine International Trade Center
511 Congress Street, ZIP: 04101
t: (207) 541-7400   *f:* (207) 541-7420

MARYLAND - BALITMORE

Michael Keaveny, Director
World Trade Center, Suite 2432
401 East Pratt Street, ZIP: 21202
t: (410) 962-4539   *f:* (410) 962-4529

A3

MASSACHUSETTS - BOSTON
Frank J. O'Connor, Director
164 Northern Avenue
World Trade Center, Suite 307, ZIP: 02210
t: (617) 424-5990   *f:* (617) 424-5992

MICHIGAN - DETROIT
Neil Hesse, Director
211 W. Fort Street, Suite 2220, ZIP: 48226
t: (313) 226-3650   *f:* (313) 226-3657

MINNESOTA - MINNEAPOLIS
Ronald E. Kramer, Director
45 South 7th St., Suite 2240, ZIP: 55402
t: (612) 348-1638   *f:* (612) 348-1650

MISSISSIPPI
Mississippi - Harrison Ford, Manager
704 East Main St., Raymond, MS, ZIP: 39154
t: (601) 857-0128   *f:* (601) 857-0026

MISSOURI - ST LOUIS
Randall J. LaBounty, Director
8182 Maryland Avenue, Suite 303, ZIP: 63105
t: (314) 425-3302   *f:* (314) 425-3381

MONTANA
Missoula, Montana - Mark Peters, Manager
c/o Montana World Trade Center
Gallagher Business Bldg., Suite 257, ZIP: 59812
t: (406) 243-2098   *f:* (406) 243-5259

NEBRASKA
Omaha, Nebraska - Meredith Bond, Manager
11135 "O" Street, ZIP: 68137
t: (402) 221-3664   *f:* (402) 221-3668

A3

NEVADA
Reno, Nevada - Jere Dabbs, Manager
1755 East Plumb Lane, Suite 152, ZIP: 89502
t: (702) 784-5203   *f:* (702) 784-5343

NEW HAMPSHIRE
Portsmouth, New Hampshire - Susan Berry, Manager
17 New Hampshire Avenue, ZIP: 03801-2838
t: (603) 334-6074   *f:* (603) 334-6110

NEW JERSEY
Trenton, New Jersey - Rod Stuart, Director
3131 Princeton Pike, Bldg. #4, Suite 105, ZIP: 08648
t: (609) 989-2100   *f:* (609) 989-2395

NEW MEXICO
New Mexico - Sandra Necessary, Manager
c/o New Mexico Dept. of Economic Development
P.O. Box 20003, Santa Fe, ZIP: 87504-5003
FEDEX:1100 St. Francis Drive, ZIP: 87503
t: (505) 827-0350   *f:* (505) 827-0263

NEW YORK - NEW YORK
John Lavelle, Acting Director
6 World Trade Center, Rm. 635, ZIP: 10048
t: (212) 466-5222   *f:* (212) 264-1356

NORTH CAROLINA - CAROLINAS
Roger Fortner, Director
521 East Morehead Street, Suite 435, Charlotte, ZIP:
28202
t: (704) 333-4886   *f:* (704) 332-2681

NORTH DAKOTA
Served by the Minneapolis, Minnesota Export
AssistanceCenter

A3

OHIIO - CLEVELAND
Michael Miller, Director
600 Superior Avenue, East, Suite 700
ZIP: 44114
t: (216) 522-4750   *f:* (216) 522-2235

OKLAHOMA
Oklahoma City, Oklahoma - Ronald L. Wilson, Director
301 Northwest 63rd Street, Suite 330, ZIP: 73116
t: (405) 608-5302   *f:* (405) 608-4211

OREGON - PORTLAND
Scott Goddin, Director
One World Trade Center, Suite 242
121 SW Salmon Street, ZIP: 97204
t: (503) 326-3001   *f:* (503) 326-6351

PENNSYLVANIA - PHILADELPHIA
Rod Stuart, Acting Director
615 Chestnut Street, Ste. 1501, ZIP: 19106
t: (215) 597-6101   *f:* (215) 597-6123

PUERTO RICO
San Juan, Puerto Rico (Hato Rey) - Vacant, Manager
525 F.D. Roosevelt Avenue, Suite 905
ZIP: 00918
t: (787) 766-5555   *f:* (787) 766-5692

RHODE ISLAND
Providence, Rhode Island - Vacant, Manager
One West Exchange Street, ZIP: 02903
t: (401) 528-5104   *f:* (401) 528-5067

SOUTH CAROLINA
Columbia, South Carolina - Ann Watts, Director
1835 Assembly Street, Suite 172, ZIP: 29201
t: (803) 765-5345   *f:* (803) 253-3614

A3

SOUTH DAKOTA

Siouxland, South Dakota - Cinnamon King, Manager
Augustana College, 2001 S. Summit Avenue
Room SS-44, Sioux Falls, ZIP: 57197
t: (605) 330-4264   *f:* (605) 330-4266

TENNESSEE

Memphis, Tennessee - Ree Russell, Manager
Buckman Hall, 650 East Parkway South, Suite 348
ZIP: 38104.
t: (901) 323-1543   *f:* (901) 320-9128

TEXAS - DALLAS

 LoRee Silloway, Director
P.O. Box 420069, ZIP: 75342-0069
2050 N. Stemmons Fwy., Suite 170, ZIP: 75207
t: (214) 767-0542   *f:* (214) 767-8240

UTAH

Salt Lake City, Utah - Stanley Rees, Director
324 S. State Street, Suite 221, ZIP: 84111
t: (801) 524-5116   *f:* (801) 524-5886

VERMONT

Montpelier, Vermont - Susan Murray, Manager
National Life Building, Drawer 20, ZIP: 05620-0501
t: (802) 828-4508   *f:* (802) 828-3258

VIRGINIA

Richmond, Virginia - Helen D. Lee Hwang, Manager
400 North 8th Street, Suite 540, ZIP: 23240-0026
P.O. Box 10026
t: (804) 771-2246   *f:* (804) 771-2390

WASHINGTON - SEATTLE

David Spann, Director
2001 6th Ave, Suite 650, ZIP: 98121
t: (206) 553-5615   *f:* (206) 553-7253

A3

WEST VIRGINIA
Charleston, West Virginia - Harvey Timberlake, Director
405 Capitol Street, Suite 807, ZIP: 25301
t: (304) 347-5123   *f:* (304) 347-5408

WISCONSIN
Milwaukee, Wisconsin - Paul D. Churchill, Director
517 E. Wisconsin Avenue, Room 596, ZIP: 53202
t: (414) 297-3473   *f:* (414) 297-3470

WYOMING
Served by the Denver, Colorado U.S. Export Assistance
Center

A3

Training and Development Solutions
for the Middle East

SDT

www.sdt.com.sa

Group 4 Securicor

almajalG4S is the largest security company in the Kingdom of Saudi Arabia. With its head office and incident control room in Jeddah it operates out of 15 branches throughout the Kingdom. Employing over 4000 staff, it is ideally placed to meet all types of security needs. As holders of ISO 9002 the company operates within a total quality framework and are the only security company in the Kingdom to be accredited. All the guards are Saudi Nationals and most have a police or army background. The modern fleet of armoured and escort vehicles ensure valuables are secure. Services include cash in transit, Total ATM and cash Management, Electronic and integrated security risk management and assessment.

SYSTEMS DIVISION
almajalG4S Technical Systems has a wealth of experience and resources in security system design and recognizes the critical importance of accurate and detailed planning from the outset of every security project. Our consultants have wide ranging experience in a variety of industries and security applications.

G4S has its own manufacturing units in the UK and owns a number of high end products such as Hisec and Mulimax systems. As a world leader in providing security solutions almajalG4S has access to the G4S world of security solutions.

A World of Security Solutions

Our services include:
- Guarding Services
- Cash in Transit
- ATM & Cash Processing
- Intelligent Security and ESecurity systems
- Access Control & CCTV
- X-Ray and metal detection equipment
- Intrusion and Perimeter detection
- Fire detection, suppression and protection systems

Contact us:
Head Office: Jeddah: 02 665 2800
Riyadh: 01 477 2145
Eastern Province: 03 846 0480

www.almajalg4s.com

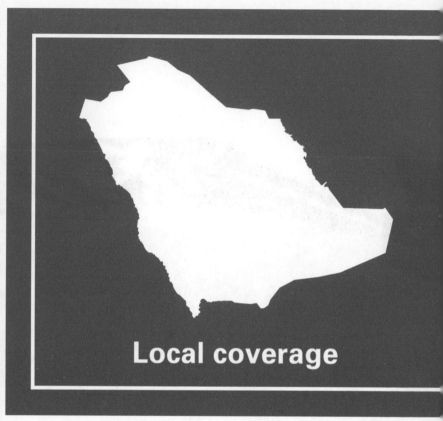

Local coverage

Global network

The Saudi British Bank (SABB) has changed its look to underline our longstanding association with **HSBC** ◆.

73 local offices and 9800 international offices are working together for you.

Local vision, international expertise

On 1 September 2005 bmi commenced a three times weekly service from London Heathrow to Riyadh. From 18 May 2006 bmi commenced a three times a week service from London Heathrow to Jeddah bmi is the only British carrier to serve the Saudi Arabian capital, offering a choice of two award-winning cabins, **the business and economy.** Customers travelling in **the business** will be able to experience top quality food prepared by bmi's on-board chef, whilst passengers in both cabins will share in the highest quality of service.

the business
as good as it gets first class service at a business fare

- dedicated check-in facilities.
- access to business lounges offering complimentary drinks, snacks and business facilities
- up to 70" legroom, 140 degrees recline
- priority boarding
- seats have adjustable footrests, headrests and lumbar support
- individual DVD player with choice of films and TV programming

on-board chef
a fully qualified chef to make the journey even more enjoyable

This service, available in the business, offers food to the highest restaurant standard. You can choose from the extensive a la carte menus available and let the highly trained chef do the rest.

economy
great value for money

- up to 33" legroom, adjustable headrests, footrests and lumbar support
- a choice of international and modern cuisine
- complimentary comfort kit*
- in-flight entertainment including movies, TV programmes, plus audio channels

bmi is proud of this award winning long haul service for more information visit flybmi.com

* on flights operating from Riyadh and Jeddah to London Heathrow

bmi
A STAR ALLIANCE MEMBER

Riyadh and Jeddah direct with bmi

bmi

- 3 non-stop flights per week
- full-service British Carrier

For more information contact your travel agent or call:

Riyadh tel: (01) 211-8014 / 211-8148

Jeddah tel: (02) 668-9950

  email: bmisales@NFS-KSA.com

  www.flybmi.com

those who know fly bmi